Through A Child's Eyes

Author Phillis T. Forrest

PRINTED IN THE UNITED STATES OF AMERICA

First edition published 2012

ISBN-13: 9781475060508

ISBN-10: 1475060505

Cover Designer: Gwendolyn C. Forrest

Editor: Tiffany K. Forrest

Advertising manager: Tyra K. Hawthorne

Author: Phillis T. Forrest

Website: www.throughachildseyes290611.com

Facebook: Author Phillis T. Forrest

Twitter: @AuthorPTForrest

Email: throughachildseyes2012@gmail.com

I dedicate my book to all the babies that slept in my nightmare. I dedicate this book to all the children that have lived or are living my nightmare. I dedicate this book to my daughters who became my soldiers and I honor them to the fullest.

Introduction

I have always known from the beginning that I would eventually tell my story. I began writing several years ago; when I thought I was ready. However, I gave up after the first try because I didn't feel inspired. I didn't want to tell the typical sexual abuse story that concentrated primarily on how the victim suffered through the physical, mental and emotional pain of the abuse. Too often these narratives relate the downward spiral of the victims as they seek out self-destructive behaviors to relieve the pain of abuse.

Within the last year, my daughter Tiffany asked, "Why haven't you started your book?" I said, "I don't know about writing it; do I really want to tell my business? What impact will I have on others by sharing my nightmare that so many have?" I felt like Moses when he was talking to God about his insecurities to be able to make an impact. (Exodus 4:10-14) I always felt that I had a purpose. I knew it was something that I was supposed to be doing. I knew my life was meant to serve a purpose. I believed that my sanity was spared and there was a reason that I did not go crazy. I wondered why he spared my sanity. Why did he give me the ability to love my babies regardless of their conception; while so many have loved theirs less? Why was I able to have relationships, give my heart and trust to those that I felt was deserving of it? There was something inside of me that was so deep that I needed to give it a voice. He gave me the gift to speak to people and they listened. I got on my knees and prayed about these perplexing questions and he answered. I was instructed to tell my nightmare as a lesson. I was to tell my story

Through A Child's Eyes as a young girl who was put in a position to be taken advantage of because her mother, her protector allowed herself to be manipulated.

I wanted to write this story in a form that would help abused victims let go of their pain a little at a time. In some sense we have all been abused and damaged in some form or fashion. "Damaged kids make damaged adults". I want victims to know that you can get past your anger and animosity. "How" you ask? By not letting your abuser win. You do this by not owning the blame and opening your heart to the good people that God sends to your life and embracing them. You do this by digging deep inside of you and finding that person that you're destined to become. You do this by loving yourself.

PROLOGUE

I decided to write this book because many children are carrying the pain of rape and molestation due to a lack of protection. It is the manipulation of my story that makes it unique. This wasn't a situation where I was snatched by someone, attacked by an uncle while everyone slept or threatened. I processed my situation differently because of the diabolical manner in which it was executed. My story exposes a predator who was patient, manipulative and supposedly a God fearing man. My story is about a man who became a part of my family and destroyed family bonds that were embedded in us since birth.

I want to reach out to the mothers, talk to them and shake them awake. I want them to accept and deal with the fact that these kinds of crimes exist. I want mothers to understand that they are the targets. It's very easy for a single mother to be targeted because she has so many titles for a man to occupy. An older man that comes into her life might serve as a father figure she never had. A man can come into her life as a companion. He can pretend to be interested in being a male role model for her fatherless son. He can offer handyman or mechanical service in order to establish a rapport with the mother.

~~~~~~~

I remember the day my life changed from; what I considered normal. It was a Sunday night and my two year old daughter had just returned home with Stephan. After giving her a bath I laid her on the bed and started to lotion her down when she said to me "Daddy put his poo in Katie poo and put his poo in my poo". Katie was one of the little girls that came over to visit regularly that I found to be one of Stephan's victims. As the blood rushed to my feet I walked into the living room and told her father what she told me. Instantly he denied it and tried to explain to me that she just loves her daddy and that sometimes a little girl will fantasize about their daddy in a romantic way. *Did I mention she was two at the time?*

At that point I realized that these were my babies and it was my job to protect them from the man that had his way with me and controlled my life for fourteen years. I tossed and turned all night thinking of a plan to protect my daughter. The next day I was in school crying when a voice in my head said "KILL HIM!" I went home with vengeance in my heart, never taking into consideration that if I had killed him and went to jail I would not have anyone to care for my babies. I was 18 years old and I didn't have the maturity or experience that it took for me to examine the situation or think about the consequences of my actions.

I walked into the house and he was asleep on the couch. I had not decided on my weapon of choice yet but I remembered thinking of getting a butcher knife and stabbing him. Before I could finish my thought there was a knock on the door. I opened the door and a heavy set dark skinned guy with big pink lips asked "Is Stephan here?" I walked into the living room and told Stephan someone was at the door for him. He asked me who was at the door and I responded, "I have no idea". As he got up off the couch and walked to the door half asleep I became annoyed that my plan to cut his penis off and watch him bleed to death was ruined. I had already pictured giving myself up willingly to the police with a smirk on my face. I turned to see what was going on at the door and all I saw were white socks being snatched out of the door. This huge guy grabbed Stephan by his neck, snatched him out the door and dragged him down the stairs into a waiting car. Another guy that was just as big as the guy that knocked on the door was standing next to the car. Stephan was shoved into the car and sandwiched in between both men. Without knowing, but knowing, I knew exactly why that drama just went down...............

CHAPTER ONE
IN THE BEGINNING

I still remember the day I met him. We were living on Clements off of Davison and Dexter Avenue. It was a sunny, pleasant afternoon and my mom called us in the house to meet her new friend; a man named Stephan. Stephan was nineteen years-old. He was a nice looking guy with medium dark brown complexion, slanted eyes, full lips, very clean cut, medium muscular build and bow-legged. He was dressed in slacks and a crisp white shirt with a tie; looking like a church boy who could have had Bible in hand. But from day one I did not like him. He gave me an eerie feeling behind his very friendly smile and those perfect teeth. When I was forced to speak to him I felt very small and uncomfortable. I walked over to him very slowly with my face in my t-shirt and when I looked up to say hi he looked down my shirt. I was seven years old at the time and oblivious to the fact that this stranger would try to change the person that I was destined to become.

Before he came into the picture my mom had gotten in trouble with Child Protective Services for leaving us alone in the house while she went to school for her G.E.D. In those days you didn't have a babysitter; your oldest sister was the babysitter. My oldest sister was 11, my second oldest sister was 9, I was 7 and my little brother was 5. So one night, while my mom was in class, we were upstairs throwing ice off the balcony of our two-family flat. One of our neighbors across the street called the police and told them that my mom had left her kids alone and we were throwing matches off the balcony. This woman already had it out for my mother anyway. My mother was 25 years old, she was attractive, independent and a hard working woman. She dressed well, carried herself like a lady and she did not associate with anyone other than our next door neighbor, who kept her eye on us when she knew my mother was not home. My mother worked and went to school. She did not drink, do drugs or go out with her friends. The lady across the street was usually nice to us when we played with her kids but one day my oldest sister overheard her call my mother a whore. Since that day the woman began to pick with my sister saying she was disrespectful; which we knew was not true because my sister was the sweetest of all of us. The real problem was that her husband paid my mother too much attention. He would break his neck to speak to her or make sure he was outside when she walked down the street. He constantly offered her rides; which she respectfully turned down every time. This man was very unattractive. He reminded me of Rog from the 70's sitcom "What's Happening" and his wife was an ugly female version of him, glasses and all. My mother had absolutely no interest in him.

The neighbor called the police and they came and took us to the police station. When my mother got home she walked into an empty house and became frantic. The neighbor next door told her what happened and then drove her to the police station. I was sitting on the policeman's desk when my mom came in. Only because she got there before Child Protective Services was she allowed to take us home, pending an investigation whether she was a working mother and that she really was at school. Through the investigation they saw that we were clean and healthy, we attended school regularly and we were all pretty good students. They also spoke to the neighbors who described my mom as being a great mother. Child Protective Services decided to close the investigation but instructed my mom to find an adequate babysitter. Soon thereafter she met Stephan and she thought he was godsend.

Back in the day sexual abuse was something that was seldom discussed. Society was not ready to digest the reality that this kind of predator was amongst us. People quickly turned a blind eye on sexual predators and refused to acknowledge the suffering of the kids that surrounded them. There weren't any T.V. shows that touched this subject. No books written, no articles in the newspaper or anything reported on the news. Sexual abuse was not an uncommon situation. So many women lived this reality as a child but still turned a blind eye as an adult. My mom was no exception.

2

The day we met Stephan turned out to be a very fun filled day. Stephan turned out to be a big kid. He played two square, jumped rope and got in the grass and wrestled with us. We thought he was the coolest and all of our friends loved him as well. After that we saw him every day.

Knowing what I know now it was all a set up. He handpicked my mother and to him she was perfect. She was a single mom with four children, she was in school and she worked a lot. He thought she was a GOLD MINE! Even though my mom was smart she was still naïve, inexperienced and desperate for help. He played his game real smooth. He watched her; basically stalked her without her knowledge. He waited for the perfect time to set up an accidental meeting. She saw him around quite often and eventually they got on speaking terms. Then one day he decided to follow her home. Almost to her house she spotted him and stopped to playfully tease him about following her home. Even to this day my mother would never forget the first question he ever asked, even before he asked her name. "DO YOU HAVE ANY KIDS?"

"Pay attention to the man that comes right in trying to get really friendly with your kids"

You should never allow your kids to get too friendly with any of your friends without monitoring that relationship. Your child lacks the maturity and experience to know what is right and wrong. In those days a child had no voice. If an adult told you to do something you did it or there were consequences. They whooped you and then took you home and your mama whooped you again. My mother had her own rules that she lived by and we suffered the consequences when she broke all of them and allowed this man into our lives.

Rule # 1: Just because someone was her friend did not make them our friend. If we saw her friends on the street we were not allowed to talk to them and her friends were told that they were not allowed to approach us if they saw us because we were not going to speak.

Rule #2: We were not allowed to answer the door for anyone when she was not home even if it was an aunt or an uncle and she made that clear to them as well.

Rule #3: No one was allowed in the house when she was not there.

Rule #4: We played with kids not adults.

Rule #5: We were not allowed to accept anything from anybody. If she had a friend over and they wanted to give us a quarter we had to be clear it with her first.

She broke all her rules when she met Stephan who in our minds made him okay and family.

CHAPTER TWO

THE COURTSHIP

I remember from the beginning that Stephan focused mainly on me. If we were playing two square in the street and I missed the ball and got out he would say something like "Awww, my baby got out," and convinced the other kids not to put me out of the game and to give me another chance because I was so small. Eventually he began calling me his little girlfriend which meant I got special treatment. He would hold my hand when we went places and put me on his shoulders if I was tired of walking. He would always defend me when I got into arguments with my sisters. He even lied to my mother when it was my fault so my mom wouldn't whoop me.

As the days, weeks and months went by this man became a part of our existence. He came over every day to eat dinner with us and he was there bright and early the next day to have breakfast with us. We were very happy to see him and my mom loved him. She even started calling him her little brother, so of course we started introducing him as our uncle. He bought us ice cream when the ice cream truck came by and he was really goofy. He would bump his head then pretend that he became a zombie and chased us. He was not like any other adult that really didn't give children the time of day.

There were a lot of times when I didn't want to be bothered with Stephan. I would be playing outside with my friends and when he came down the street he expected me to stop playing with my friends and run up to him to acknowledge his presence. I wanted him to go upstairs and talk to my Mom like other adults. I started feeling a sense of obligation to him because he called me his little girlfriend and that is how he wanted me to act. He would expect me to sit on his lap and interact with him the whole time he was there. Thankfully, my mother was the type that didn't have adult conversations around kids. My mom would send me back outside scolding me, saying that I was sitting under him. I pretended to pout like it really mattered to me but I was really happy as hell. I could count on good 'ole mom to get me back outside with my sisters and brother.

I felt like he had a crush on me like the little boys at school. I would get treated special and could get what I wanted out of them, like candy and second chances at games. I even became bossy and demanding because I knew he would give me my way, just like I did with the other seven year old boys. Sometimes I would get an attitude and be mean to get my way because he was so eager to please me. But sometimes I was being mean because I didn't want to be bothered with him because he was always in my face. After spending some time in the house with my mom he would find some reason to come outside to play with us. Later he would find some way to say we had to rest so I could sit on his lap. I would think to myself, "I'm seven years old, I don't need to rest!" When my mom didn't see me playing she would come to find me. I was blamed again for being on his lap. She would say to him: "Stop spoiling her!" I was accustomed to my mom being straightforward. I was waiting for the day that she would tell him not to put me on his lap anymore. But she never did. I was not even allowed to sit on my uncle's or auntie's lap. She allowed this man to constantly put me on his lap even though I didn't like it. He was an adult and I was a kid and I was not allowed to speak my mind.

I really didn't like sitting on his lap because he was interfering with what I really wanted to do and that was playing outside with all the other kids. But he made me feel *obligated* because to him I was his little girlfriend.

~~~~~

<u>Never let anyone label your child. (Ex. This is my little girlfriend)</u> **MOTHERS! Do not allow an adult to label your child with a title that is not age appropriate. Your child does not have the life experience to understand the meaning behind certain titles. Your child will start to feel obligated to pay this person attention or live up to that title. Stephan took the title "girlfriend" literally and expected me to perform as such.**

MOTHERS! Keep your children off of a man's lap. He is getting aroused with the act itself. Ask yourself these questions:

What do you feel when you sit on your man's lap? Why do strippers make so much money off of lap dances?

Kids are constantly moving so he is getting a level of excitement that your child is not even aware of. Once again my mom has broken another rule.

Rule #6: No sitting on anybody's lap!

~~~~~~~

2

Stephan was eventually allowed to come over when my mother wasn't there, which was something that she had never allowed before. One day he was cooking dinner for us and he claimed that we were in need of some items and sent my two sisters and brother to the store. I was told to stay behind. He called me into the bathroom and sat me on his lap and started to tell me that I was his little girlfriend. He kissed me on my cheek and then kissed me on the lips. I didn't think much of it because my mom kissed us on our lips all the time. He told me because we were boyfriend and girlfriend that it was all right. He told me that he was going to give me a bath because I wasn't going back outside; which made me mad because it was the middle of the day. I became combative and said, "My mama said I could go outside when you were here," and I told him I wasn't taking a bath. My sisters and brother returned from the store and was knocking on the door. He purposely sent them back to the store saying that they did not get the correct brand he specifically needed so the food would taste right. They left to go back to the store and he came back in the bathroom to take off my clothes to give me a bath. I told him that I was seven and I could take my own bath but he said that he wanted to make sure I was clean because I wasn't taught how to properly bathe. I don't remember being uncomfortable about this because I don't even think I knew to be. After my bath he laid me on the bed and started to lotion me down while convincing me that I was his baby so it was all right. He then undressed and lay on top of me. I remember being paralyzed wondering, "What the hell!" My sisters and brother returned back from the store and once again he told them that he changed his mind and that he tried to catch them to add something to the list. I had put on my pajamas by then and my sister asked me why was I in my pajamas. I said, "Stephan told me I had to stay in the house". My sister reiterated to him that my mother allowed us to go outside when he was there. He got upset and said that after dinner we were all taking a bath and staying in the house when they got back from the store so they better enjoy going to the store. Of course, this made my sisters and brother really take their time returning back from the store on the 3rd trip. I was pissed and I acted very defiantly. When he tried to remove my pajamas I told him NO! He reminded me that my mother had instructed me to do as he said and if I didn't, I would get a whooping when she got home and I said "SO"! He then threatened to call my mother so I said "CALL HER"! He picked up the phone and I became scared, which almost made me pee on myself because I knew I was going to get it when my mother got home. He started talking into the phone and said "Yeah, Sophia". I cried out and said "ok I will do it"! He then said "I was calling to tell you that Toni was being a really good girl" and hung up. When I got older I asked my mother about that conversation; I was not shocked that she had no idea what I was talking about. He never called her.

He took me back in the bedroom and laid on top of me. He told me if I did this I could put my clothes back on and go outside when my sisters and brother got back and he would buy me ice cream when the truck came by. To a seven year old that made a lot of sense. When he was done I had all this white stuff on my stomach that I thought was lotion. I walked around for years wondering where the lotion came from. I even got in trouble later because I told my little brother that if we rubbed our bellies together we could make lotion. I laid on top of him and we rubbed our bellies together but nothing happened. My mother walked in the room and caught us. I was really confused why she beat the crap out of both of us and went on and on about we were sister and brother and that we do not do things like that. The whole time I was thinking "I was just trying to show him how we can make lotion". If my mother would have calmed down for half a second and talked to me she would have understood what I was doing; which could have led to questions that could have made my life different.

CHAPTER THREE

When I was 9 years old my mom sent us to stay with my grandmother for a year. This would be our first time meeting her and being in Aiken, South Carolina. My mom needed to work two jobs so she could buy a house. She promised that when we got back we would have a new house. My grandmother was a burly dark skinned woman with big breasts and no butt. She had a big chicken booty looking nose and she looked like James Brown in the face with the same hairstyle and everything. I had an uncle named Dwayne who was the same age as me. He was a spoiled, whining bully and we did not get along at all.

My grandmother was such a character. She was evil, mean and I did not like her but I was respectful. My grandmother was the type that loved her kids based on how much she loved each child's daddy. She had 11 children and if she didn't like your daddy you got the beat down, but if she loved your daddy you got treated as good as gold. Dwayne was a result of the love of her life, Eric Brown. He was so ugly. He was a dark black country boy who stood about 5'9", skinny and looked like a dried up raisin. And he was married! His wife would come over and she and my grandmother would have it out right in the middle of the street. Now my grandma was no punk and she always put a whooping on his wife. My grandma was only 44 years old at the time.

My uncle Dwayne was allowed to treat us anyway he wanted; he could hit us, bite us and kick us. We were not allowed to do anything about it; so he thought. But I was from the D and we didn't take a butt whooping, we gave them out! Since he was my age and my sister was a lot scarier than me I took care of him when he thought he was going to bully any of us. I got a whooping *everyday* for it! But that was ok because the next time I made sure I took it out on him when we got into it. Eventually he got tired of fighting with me so he left us alone. He would argue with me but he dared not hit any of us. Mama's rule was always that I couldn't pass the first lick but I could protect myself.

My grandmother's favoritism towards Dwayne was very obvious. She would buy him McDonalds for dinner and he would tease us because we had to eat beans and cornbread. The school year was over and we were supposed to spend the summer there and go home at the end of the season. Well, that didn't happen! On the last day of school Dwayne was in one of his picking moods because my grandmother brought him McDonalds again. I shoved my plate and it fell on the floor and I yelled, "I'm tired of eating this shit!" and of course Dwayne ran and told Grandma.

My grandma came into the kitchen and said, "What did you say", thinking I was going to back down. I told her exactly what I said. I told her I was tired of eating this shit and that it was unfair for Dwayne to eat McDonald's and we had to eat beans all the time. Since my sisters and I had discussed this situation before I turned to them assuming that they would cut in and agree with what I was saying. I continued; "You treat him better than you treat us, don't she Gennifer and Jadon?" These heifers didn't say a word and started eating their beans like it was steak and potatoes. I humped my shoulders thinking, Oh well you can't unring the bell, so I just finished what I had to say. I screamed, "I want to go home!" Even though we were not due home until the end of August that little altercation got us home by that Sunday. GOOD RIDDANCE!

2

When we got back to Detroit my mother had bought us a home just like she said. It was a four bedroom bungalow with two bathrooms, a basement and a nice size back yard. We loved it and I was so happy to see my mother. My grandma told my mother about the incident but my mom didn't get upset because she knew how my grandma was, having been treated the same way.

My grandma disliked my mother's dad because he saw her for the whore she was and divorced her and married Big Mama. To be spiteful, my grandma sent my Aunt Ester, Uncle Jim and my mom to live with their dad and his new wife. They were so happy and so was Granddaddy and Big Momma. After a period of time Grandma was breeding babies like roaches so she made my mother and her siblings come home to take care of her children. I think, to this day that never set right with my mom. With their father they lived well, dressed well and ate every day but with my grandma they lived in a shack, with no furniture and with whatever man she was laid up with at the time.

3

Toward the end of the summer we were instructed to go meet Stephan at the Grand River bus stop; which was 3 blocks up from where we lived. It turned out Stephan was coming to live with us. We were happy to see him because he was like family and we did love him a lot.

While we were away he had joined the army. We didn't have a problem with him coming to live with us and my mom was relieved because now someone would be there with us while she was at both of her jobs. At this time Gennifer was 14, Jadon was 12, I was 10, and my brother was 7.

Stephan was a really good cook. He would cook for us, kept the house clean and made sure my mother didn't have anything to do when she got home. But things were not perfect. Within a matter of days he started on me again. I would get an attitude because he would find ways to keep me in the house. Whenever he tried to do anything like kiss or hug on me we would fight like we were both kids. My mom would come home fussing asking me what we fought about. I would tell my mother it was because he always had some reason for me to come in the house and I wanted to stay outside and play. Stephan claimed I was in the house for acting up outside and he made me come in the house. Coming home so many times to Stephan and I fighting my mother began to allow Stephan to discipline us. BIG MISTAKE!

Stephan started whooping me constantly for not kissing him, cuddling with him or sitting on his lap. He constantly reminded me of my mother's words about how I was supposed to do what he said. It was strange because I never respected him as an adult. To me, he was a pesty boyfriend that followed me around and wouldn't leave me alone. If I was over my friend Ciara's house, he would walk over there and make me come home for absolutely nothing so we would fight. He would try to whoop me but I wasn't having it so I would become very defiant. I would cuss at him, fall on the floor and kick him. My mom would come home to another one of our big fights. I would jump up and run to tell her my side of the story and he was right behind me trying to tell his story like my brother and I did when we fought. "Mama I was around Ciara's house and he came around there bothering me for nothing. He's always finding a reason to keep me in the house with him. He makes me sick!" He began to lie "I told Toni to do something and she told me she wasn't going to do it. She went around to Ciara's house after I told her not to go outside until it was done!" My mother thought I was being hardheaded and she would whoop me, which gave him more power because she would say, "If I come home again and he has any more complaints about you, you are going to get it again!" All I could think was that my mom was making me obey a man who was forcing me to be in a relationship with him and all I wanted to be was a kid and go outside and play.

Ciara had a couple of gangster cousins that stayed in trouble; they couldn't stand Stephan. One day he came over Ciara's house bothering me and they beat him up, just off of G.P. (general purposes). They busted his lip, gave him a black eye and broke his arm. TEE HEE!

NEVER GIVE ANYONE PERMISSION TO

DISCIPLINE YOUR CHILD

Allowing a person to discipline your children gives them too much power. They will take that and your words and use it against your child. They instill fear in your child because they have your permission to hurt them. My mother never allowed anyone to discipline us, not even our relatives. Once again she's extending permission to him and broke her rules.

Rule #7: No one is allowed to put their hands on you but me.

If you put this person in an authoritative position with your consent the child is rendered helpless and has no choice but to obey this person because their mother gave permission.

4

At bed time my mom slept upstairs and Stephan was allowed to sleep in our general area. He would sleep in my room with me and my brother but slept in my bed. He would feel on me, kiss on me, and lay me on top of him. I would act like I was asleep and laid there like a limp noodle until he just gave up. He knew I was faking, so just like any man that wants sex from his woman and she wouldn't give into his desires, the next day he really made my life hell. He started bright and early. He started complaining, telling my mother I "got smart" when I didn't. He would say he told me to do something and I didn't do it. By the time my mom left for work I would be on punishment. Now that my mother worked two jobs, Stephan had complete access to me and he slept in my bed.

ALLOWING ACCESS TO YOUR CHILD

MOTHERS! Most of the time, this abuse is being done right under your nose under your own roof. In my situation, this was Stephan's intentions all along. He was waiting to gain my mother's trust to gain total access to us. He should have never

been allowed in our general area. If she was going to rent the basement to him then the door to the basement should have been locked at all times to separate us, especially if she was going to sleep two floors up.

~~~~~~

Stephan was a big joke to me. That's why I disrespected him. I felt we were on the same level. I stayed in trouble about my attitude and my big mouth. I would make a decision to get a whooping if it was worth it to me and fighting him was worth it because he irritated me. Even though he was molesting me I didn't know to tell anyone. This has been my relationship with him since we met him. It wasn't like he was hurting me, and afterwards I could go back outside and he brought me ice cream. To me, he wronged me by not letting me go outside to play with my friends. In so many ways I was telling my mother what he was doing to me but she never stopped to even think about it. I told her how he always made me come in the house when she would leave. He would find reasons to make me stay in the house with him. She never once questioned his obsession with me. She never put her foot down with him or enforced any other rule. Instead, she allowed him to dictate my punishment. However, my oldest sister did question him when she noticed I wasn't outside with them? But all he had to say was, "you're going to stay in the house next!" That was enough for her and she would go back outside. At least she tried. When Gennifer was 14 years-old she had a conversation with my mother about Stephan making me come in the house every time she left, even though I had done nothing wrong. My mom's response was same as always; that she left him in charge when she was away and for my sister to stay in a child's place. But Gennifer didn't back down. She wanted my mother to know that he was trying to monopolize me when she was away. My sister could not stand him, but mama gave him the power so she was powerless. My mother knew I was not disrespectful to adults. She should have questioned why I stood toe-to-toe with this man and argued with him like I was his equal. She should have questioned why a grown man would argue with a child like I was his woman. My sisters and brother started treating him the same way until my mom would jump in and side with him.

CHAPTER FOUR

Stephan eventually moved out into a two family flat on a street called Ilene, off of Wyoming and Fenkell. He lived upstairs from his landlord and her family. She had older children that didn't live at home. The three children at home ranged from 9 years old to 20 years old.

We would all go over to his house for a sleep-over. There were other kids as well. There was June; she was 14, her six year old little brother Rico and Kim who was nine from down stairs. At the end of the day we would take our baths, but even though our mother would pack our pajamas everyone had to put on one of his big t-shirts with nothing under them. I always had to sleep in the bed with him even though I wanted to sleep on the floor in the living room with the other kids. Stephan would roll around on the floor with us and wrestle and tickle us and we would have a ball.

~~~~~~~~

Rule #8, my mother NEVER! EVER! EVER! EVER allowed us to spend the night with anyone! We were not allowed to go to slumber parties. We weren't even allowed in our friend's houses PERIOD. When my friend went inside her house to use the bathroom, I sat on the porch. My mother better not had heard of me being inside of my friend's house.

~~~~~~~

After a while Stephan stopped coming to get my two older sisters and just came to get me and my little brother. His excuse was that Gennifer and Jadon were in high school and they had all their sports and friends. Soon he stopped coming to get my younger brother and was just coming to get me.

Rule #9: If someone asked to take any of us anywhere, just one couldn't go. If one went, all of us had to go!

~~~~~~~

His landlord who lived downstairs had a daughter named Brenda who was 20. She was a thick, juicy woman but she was nicely built. She was very funny and I really liked her. Every day we would go downstairs and have dinner with the family because Stephan had a knack for blending in with the families. I would spend days with Stephan without seeing my mother or even talking to her. I hated to see night coming because I knew I had to go to bed and he would feel on me, grind and make lotion.

Brenda had a boyfriend named Kirk and she eventually became pregnant with her first born named Sweetie. I loved this baby and she was so pretty. She had a fair complexion, beautiful hair, with a little mole that I thought was so cute above her little full lips. I remember Brenda and Kirk arguing because he couldn't stand Stephan and he had a problem with his daughter being in this man's presence. He saw the predator in him. Kirk constantly told Brenda that Stephan was messing with her little sister Kim, and he didn't trust him. She would stand up for Stephan and say that he was jealous of him which was what Stephan told her when she brought Kirk's accusation to his attention. Stephan told Brenda he probably thought they were sleeping together that is why he was telling lies on him. Eventually Kirk and Brenda broke up because she wouldn't give up Stephan. That was exactly what Stephan wanted and now she too was at his mercy. Stephan had a way of running every man away. Throughout my story you will see that all the mothers in my story became his loyal followers like they were in a cult or something.

Everything I did lead to Stephan bumping and grinding on me making lotion. If I coughed, he believed I wanted some attention from him. If I asked to go home and he said no and I got an attitude, he said it was because I was jealous that he was paying attention to some other little girl. I didn't give a damn as long as I got to go outside and play! Stephan was really attracted to me. He always complimented me. He would tell me I had pretty legs, and that my body was nice and that my skin was beautiful. I remember disliking my skin because he would lay me on the bed after my bath, lotion me down and tell me how my complexion was pretty. It always led to him bumping and grinding on me making lotion. To be honest I didn't know what he was looking at because I was not an attractive kid. I had a teaspoon of nappy hair and big lips that my sisters teased me about constantly. But I think that's why he singled me out.

~~~~~~

PAY ATTENTION WHEN ONE CHILD IS SINGLED OUT!

Just so you will know; besides attraction there are other ways a predator may seek your child out. Sometimes your child might be targeted because they are the oddball or considered a disciplinary problem. The one that everyone picks on, talks about and teases. They are singled out because it's easy to win them over. The predator will pay attention to them and treat them nice when everyone else mistreats them. This child gravitates toward them. The predator then has the security of knowing that if the child told, no one will believe them any way. MOTHERS ARE YOU GETTING THIS? IN OTHER WORDS SOMETIMES WE MAKE OUR OWN KIDS TARGETS!

~~~~~~~

2

My sisters were getting older. My sister Gennifer was 15, Jadon 13, I was 11, and my brother was 8. I came home from school and did my regular routine: chores, homework then T.V, by that time my mom would be coming in the door and I could go outside. One day Gennifer came home and I knew something was wrong because she was furious. I never saw my sister so mad because she was usually so calm. She came into the kitchen and my mom asked Gennifer, "Why is your face all torn up?" Before she could open her mouth, Stephan busted in our house and started screaming, "Sophia, she is lying, I never touched her!" We looked at him bewildered because Gennifer never said a word. He continued "I never touched her and she said she was going to lie on me". BLAH! BLAH! BLAH! Gennifer had no intentions of saying anything but since he brought it up, Gennifer said, "Yes you did! You tried to do it to me!" Before we knew it my mother hauled off and slapped the shit out of Gennifer! My mom accused her of being a liar and went on about how much he had done for us. It never dawned on me that what Stephan tried to do with my sister was what he was doing to me. I didn't know how to vouch for her. Gennifer was crying and went to her room. I went to her room and told her I was sorry. We hugged and I cried with her. I found out that he had tried to have sex with her. They got into a fight and Gennifer walked home; which was about 20 miles. Mama and Stephan talked for a few hours and he told her he was taking me home with him. She made me go. I was pissed. I wanted to stay home with my sister and I was mad at him for getting my sister slapped. So when we got to his house FIGHT 942 was on. He tried to explain to me what happened and he told me not to be jealous! He claimed that Gennifer made that up because she was jealous of our relationship. Things started really getting bad after that. When he came over Gennifer would leave the room and not speak, and then she would get in trouble for not speaking. As punishment he would make her go with him and my mama would make her go. He could pick and choose anyone of us at any given time and we had to go. I would tell him I wasn't going and he would tease me and say, "I bet you go!" He would talk to my mother for a while and the next thing I knew I was packing some pajamas that he wasn't going to let me wear anyway.

Stephan would spend hours talking to my mother about us like she didn't know her own kids. She would accept everything he said. He would tell her, "Sophia, Toni got a lot of mouth and she is

43

fast, she's going to be pregnant by 14 if you don't get a hold of her!" He told her that is why he came to get me every chance he got so he could watch over me while she was at work because she didn't need the headache. She was drinking his kool-aid big time. He showered her with compliments about how she was a great mother, how hard she worked to take care of her family and that he admired her. He told her he wouldn't do this for anyone else because he didn't want to be bothered with any kids. After that I had no choice whether I went or not. He would pick me up from school and I wouldn't go home for months. I wouldn't see my sisters and brother or my mama unless we visited. Yes, I had to visit my own home.

Stephan then started shutting me away from my family. I couldn't see my family and I didn't have any friends. My mother never called to check on me and I missed her so much. If I asked to call my mother he would say she was asleep and not to bother her. Stephan knew I idolized my mother so he started talking about her. He would say she was fake and phony. He would tell me that she didn't care about me and that was why she didn't call and that's why I was with him. He claimed that the only reason we had clothes was because he always had to lend her money. He compared how she dressed to how we dressed. He told me she only cared about herself and he was the one that made the sacrifice to go without so we could have things. I didn't know what to think. All I knew was she didn't call me and she always made me leave my home to go with him. Every time she got on us for disrespecting him she would talk about how much we should appreciate him because he did so much for our family. So I started to believe him. I began disliking my mother. Every time we would visit her, Stephan would tell her I did something wrong and she would become annoyed with me. If I asked to stay home she would say no. At this point I was living with a man at 11. After a while I adapted to this lifestyle. I believed my mom officially didn't love me anymore and that she loved him more. After all, she believed everything he said and she never listened to me. She gave me to him and then he became my family. I was always in the house so I concentrated on my schoolwork because there was nothing else to do. I was excelling in school; something Stephan manipulated my mother into believing was a result of his own guidance.

3

Stephan' obsession with me should have been so obvious to my mother. She got caught up in his compliments and it clouded her judgment. She really believed that he thought a lot of her. He had her convinced that he was really trying to help. Little did she know he was setting his trap to have full control over her and that allowed him to do whatever he wanted to her family.

He snickered at my mother. He called her dumb. I knew it was because he was playing her like a fool and he enjoyed it. He targeted my mother because she was smart but very naïve about the kind of predator he was. He figured if she was so smart; then why didn't she see his game. Stephan had his eyes set on me from the beginning and he set out to get me. If she would have opened her eyes, she would have noticed that he had too much interest in me for an adult man.

~~~~~~~

PAY ATTENTION TO THE PERSON THAT CONSTANTLY SECLUDE A CHILD

Watch the person that is focused on secluding your child. It is done purposely so your child will completely depend on him. He can start feeding your child negative information because there is no one there who is close enough for your child to confide in. The predator is only going to teach that which is beneficial to keep the child he is abusing totally at his disposal. This person constantly has something to say when the child has a chance to spend time with other people. Stephan's favorite line was, "Now Sophia, you know Toni shouldn't be going. She's going to act up. She's fast and got a big mouth!"

In my case, Stephan eventually secluded the whole family. No one liked him. My mother was quick to jump to his defense and protect him. Everyone stopped coming around out of disgust for her and because they couldn't stand the sight of him. So now we had no outsider in our circle to point out the inconsistency in his abnormal behavior. We were at his mercy.

LISTEN TO THE KEY PEOPLE IN YOUR LIFE

Everybody has someone in their life that they trust and respect their opinions. Everyone in my mom's circle said something to her about this man and she ignored them. My mother was unwilling to accept anything anybody had to say because that meant she didn't know everything. It was her pride that kept this predator in our lives. MOTHERS: LISTEN TO THE PEOPLE IN YOUR CIRCLE THAT YOU LOVE AND TRUST. LISTEN TO THE PEOPLE WHO YOU KNOW HAVE YOUR BEST INTEREST AT HEART AND WILL ALWAYS BE HONEST WITH YOU! HIND-SIGHT IS ALWAYS BETTER! Relatives and close friends would ask, "Why is Toni always with him? Why is she living with him? Who is this and where the hell did he come from?" Even people that didn't know my mother such as my friend's parents, teachers and neighbors noticed right off something wasn't right about the relationship I had with this man. My Aunt Ester would mention how he showed too much concern about me for someone that wasn't related to me. It was too much interest for a grown man to have in a young girl. LISTEN!

CHAPTER FIVE

At 13 years old I was in the 8th grade attending middle school and I was back living with my mom. Stephan had been popping in and out of my life which was fine with me. When he wasn't around I was happy that I could play with my friends and be my age. When Stephan came back around he would have a new younger child with him. The new child on the scene was Trent but Stephan had everyone call him Little Stephan. He was a sandy brown, curly haired little boy with green/grey hazel eyes and he had skin the color of butter. He was 5 years old; I loved the way he talked because he was tongue tied and sounded like Daffy Duck. His mother Carmen was a fair skinned woman that always wore heels. She had an older son named Mannie; He was about 12 years old at the time. He was a chocolate little boy with course hair. He absolutely HATED, HATED, HATED Stephan. Stephan didn't mess with Mannie because he was afraid of him. Mannie was a very defiant little boy and if his mother ever thought he was going to be respectable to Stephan, it would've been a trick to it and he made that clear to both of them. Mannie was very nice and he had a little crush on me. As much as he hated Stephan he would lurk around the corner just to see me while avoiding Stephan. Stephan knew Mannie liked me too because he always made it a point to make sure we stayed apart. Mannie was always very pleasant to me and through a silent conversation we had when I looked in his eyes, he knew what Stephan was doing to me.

Stephan had moved into a three family flat house that was a dump and Carmen lived down stairs. She was the type of woman that thought more of her self than she ought to. When you walked in her flat, she had it decorated very nicely but the house was a shabby shack. She didn't have a car, she dressed nice but not sharp. I did like her; though I always knew that she knew exactly what Stephan was doing to me but I felt like she blamed me. All the mothers had a suspicious look in their eyes about Stephan but they continuously allowed their children to go with him. Trent slept upstairs with him a lot. Stephan called him his son and Trent called him daddy. This is why Mannie didn't like him. He saw right through him and he didn't like that his mom let his little brother claim him as his father.

2

One day I was outside standing at the end of the yard. After not seeing him in a long while, Stephan strolled up. It was late August and I had on a pair of shorts with a little tank top. He made a comment that my shorts were too short and too tight. I told him to shut up and mind he own business. He grabbed me by my arm and told me I was going with him. I told him that I wasn't going anywhere so we began to fight. He tried to rip my shorts off saying that I looked like a whore. He ripped both sides of my shorts so now I look like I got on a skirt with high slits and you could see my panties. I slapped him and I dug my nails in his face. I knew I might not win this fight but he damn sure was going to look like he'd been in one! My mother was coming down the street and I ran to meet her. I told her Stephan came over messing with me. He said he was getting on me because I had all these little boys over. She sent me to my room while she talked to Stephan in the kitchen for a while. She came in my room and told me to pack my things because I was going to stay with Stephan while she went out of town. I asked, "Why do I have to go with him?" She said, "I don't trust you to act like you have any sense while I'm gone with your fast behind". Now my mother never called me or any of us fast. I was 13 and wasn't even interested in boys at the time. Stephan had been calling me fast since I was 7 years old. She accepted what he said instead of what she knew. I got very defiant and told her I wasn't going. I screamed that he make me do things I didn't want to do. She stepped in my bedroom and asked me what things? I said, "Stuff". I started crying and shaking because I was scared that she would slap me like she slapped Gennifer when she tried to tell her about Stephan's abuse. I just kept saying I don't want to go. She said if I wasn't going to tell her then I was going. By this time Stephan was coming down the hall to my room. My mom said, "Toni said you make her do things, what things?" My mouth fell open, "Mama you're really going to tell him what I said." He laughed it off and just said, "Awe Sophia you know how kids are every time they can't get their way, they say we're being mean to them." She turned to me and told me to pack my things. I grabbed my clothes and walked out of my bedroom. When I got to the end of the hallway I told her we all hated her! She slapped me and told me to get out of her house. That was the first night he penetrated me.

~~~~~~

If you want your child to talk to you, you cannot have conversation in front of the person they're having a problem with. Your child is very uncomfortable and it is important to calm down the situation and make them feel comfortable. Allow your child to speak. Show no attitude with your child like you are taking what they are saying lightly. Don't make your child prove their point! Your child is not articulate enough to stand toe to toe intellectually with an adult. If this would have been done things would have been different throughout this whole story. I told my mother verbally, physically and emotionally that something was going on and she ignored me. Even the signs that were right in front of her face she ignored. A child doesn't have the intellect to really explain what is going on especially if the parent failed to educate their child about inappropriate touches. They are very confused about what they think is right, what they feel is right and what they know is right. Stephan spent my life playing with my head and confusing me. The way my mother handled things she basically put her stamp of approval on my situation.

~~~~~~~~

Stephan didn't have a car so we walked the 8 blocks to his house. He took all these extra detours. He even went to the grocery store with my shorts ripped up. My mother never even noticed. He did this to embarrass me. He said since I wanted to act like a whore then he was going to treat me like one. He was very loud in the store making sure everyone paid attention to me. My mother had no idea the things this man was doing to her child. He took her 13 year old daughter and made her his woman against her will but with her mother's unknown support.

~~~~~~~~

3

I spent my whole 8th grade year with him. At this point he was actually having sex with me. When I didn't like it he said it was because I was gay because I was supposed to like it. He told me that this is what men and women do in a relationship and nothing was wrong with it. I didn't like it because it hurt and I would swell up so bad he would make me put a cold towel down there. He laughed and said I would get used to it. He would tell me to do things like oral sex that totally disgusted me. I kept thinking, "Ugh, you pee with that thing" and I would throw up so he didn't make me do that anymore. He constantly called me gay and said that he was going to spread it around the street and no one would be my friend.

~~~~~~~~~

It was a cold rainy day, the wind was howling. You could feel the house shaking. We stayed in the house that day and watched T.V. I noticed that every time Stephan saw me naked he would want to have sex with me so I started getting dressed in the bathroom. He started realizing I was doing that so he would come in the bathroom for something every time I took a bath. I started shutting the curtain but he would always find a reason to pull the curtain back. After that I started locking the door and when he couldn't get in we would get into a big argument. He thought that night he was going to force himself on me but I was still sore from earlier that day. He put me outside in the cold hallway with no clothes on except my panties and a t-shirt for fighting him back. It was about 11 o'clock p.m. I was balled up in the corner because I refused to beg him to come back inside. I would have walked to my mother's house if I was at least dressed but being naked I just had to stay warm the best way I could. I eventually fell asleep in the corner until about 4:00 o'clock am. A big rat came up the stairs. I started bamming on the door and begged him to let me in. He did but I had to agree to have sex with him, so I did.

~~~~~~~

I had not heard from my mother since the school year began and she had no idea what I was going through. I hadn't seen my sisters because they were out of junior high by the time I got there and my brother had not gotten there yet. This was a very confusing time for me. I was emotional and upset all the time. I was not a dummy. I knew what was being done to me wasn't right but I didn't know that this was a crime and that he could go to jail. By now I've been going though this for so long I thought it was normal and it happened to every girl. I didn't have an outlet or any one to tell me any different. Plus my mother gave me to him so I thought she had to be ok with it. I made up my mind to ask her why.

I decided to act up at school one day so my mom would have to come to my school and wouldn't you know it, here comes Stephan. He told them he was my uncle. DAMN! Stephan whooped me when I got home so now I'm really confused. You whooped me like a child but any other time you treat me like I am your woman or have me acting like a mom to Trent and Sweetie when they came over. I took care of them; I bathed them, fed them, got them ready for school and combed their hair like I had kids. I didn't really mind that part though because I did love them. I was a kid or his woman whenever it was convenient for him.

When school was out for the summer, Stephan's mother died. We took the Greyhound bus to Mobile, Alabama for her funeral. I finally found out why Stephan had such an eerie feeling about him. His brother Tee came and picked us up from the bus station. He was tall and slender, fair complexion with a short afro that looked like someone had pressed and curled it. He was attractive but dirty and bummy looking. I didn't like him. He had that same eerie feel that crawled up the back of my neck. I remembered that same feeling the day I met Stephan. We pulled up to his family's house and this house was so shabby it had to have been there since slavery. There were adults sitting on the porch drinking kool-aid out of mayonnaise jars with the label still on it, getting high and drinking beer. When we walked on the porch, I noticed these fools had a living room couch on the porch. The little house had three bedrooms and was sparsely furnished with fans in every window, (the fans weren't doing nothing but blowing the hot air around.) This house was packed to the capacity. When we walked in the door, Stephan was greeted by all his sisters and brothers. It was eight of them. It also was about ten young girls, ages ranging from 7 to 16, and three boys ages ranging

11 to 15. The brothers were handsome, tall and slender but dirty looking and they all look like they stunk. They all had their hair tied up with scarves like Morris Day. Their names were Lee, Rick, Eddie, Rome, Ron and Tee. The sisters were big boned, big breasted women with only a teaspoon of hair that was slick to the back and pretty faces. Their names were Bernice, Sal and Tiny. One thing they all had in common was they all had at least four gold teeth in their mouth. There was a bunk bed in the living room and his oldest brother Lee lay in the bed with a dirty looking white girl about 16 years old and when she rose up to move, he slapped her. But the black girl; looking about 14, sitting in the chair next to the bed was introduced as Lee's wife but was said to be Stephan's niece. HUH? I assumed because of the funeral some of these people were out of town guest. Later at bedtime I found out everyone that was in that house lived there because they all settled into their designated sleeping areas. I noticed that certain females in the house flocked to each brother. All the brothers shared the rooms with all these young girls and boys. The sisters slept in the living room with specific children too.

Stephan and I were allowed to sleep in the lower bunk bed in the living room. I was very uncomfortable; besides being hot, sticky, funky and infested with the largest roaches I had ever seen in my life; Satan lived here. I was surrounded by pimps, prostitutes, addicts, alcoholics, rapist and killers. I remember being afraid. I couldn't breathe. I never went to the bathroom or left Stephan's side. I held his hand the whole time and only let go to let our hands dry because they were getting sweaty, but I didn't let him go even then, I held him around his waist. Eventually someone asked Stephan who I was. It became clear that the environment I was in was a haven for the devil when Stephan answered that a thirteen year old girl was his wife and nobody blinked.

I didn't sleep the whole night, I was so jumpy. I thought bugs were crawling on me and I didn't feel safe. I heard all types of moaning and groaning all through the night that sound more like demonic spirits. Stephan and I had an argument because he tried to have sex with me. One of his brothers overheard us and smirked and grunted at Stephan. He did it in a way to call Stephan a punk. Stephan wanted to hit me so bad but he knew I would fight back and his family would see that he had no control plus I would talk about his whole family.

The next day was the funeral and throughout the whole funeral Stephan tried to save face in front of his brothers by talking disrespectful to me. I ignored Stephan. I was ready to go home. This was my first funeral but I still knew this wasn't right. It reminded me of the funeral scene in the movie Ray. The casket was made of hard, unfinished wood. They put their mother in a wooden box on the ground! There weren't any decorations, flowers or a ceremony. Everyone stood around cussing, fussing, drinking, getting high and a group of cousins were shooting craps against the casket. This woman had to be a terrible mother, did terrible things to her children and allowed terrible things to happen to them. At the funeral I found out that everyone in that home was blood family. The brothers and sisters had sexual relationships and babies were born. Now they have relationships with the children and the sickness continues. The mother let it happen. Stephan, the youngest, was passed around between his sisters and brothers until he was old enough to do the passing. This was the norm for Stephan. His whole family was SICK!

After the funeral, Stephan and I headed back home. I refused to sit with him and he knew not to start any shit with me because he didn't want to take a chance on what would come out of my mouth. I slept all the way home because I was so tired. I didn't get any sleep the night before.

As soon as we made it into the city, Stephan took me home. I remember walking in the house and my sisters were happy to see me but my mother just said hi and told us she wanted us to go to the store. I was so hurt. That was all I anticipated was seeing my mom and just crying. She had no idea what I went through. Stephan told my mother that he brought me home because he was tired of me. I thought to myself, "I'm tired of your ass!" He came in the back to try to kiss me good bye and I smashed his face with the palm of my hand and called him a two faced dog. I soon found out that when I had not seen my family for a long time he was coming over every day. My sisters asked me why I didn't come over when he did. I was confused. Can you believe they told me that when my mother asked him why he didn't bring me with him he told her it was because I got in trouble in school and I was being punished? HOW THE HELL AM I ON PUNISHMENT FROM SEEING MY MAMA? NOT TO MENTION, WHY ARE YOU ASKING HIM? MY MOTHER SHOULD HAVE SAID BRING MY CHILD HOME!

~~~~~~

Can you see what's going on here? My mother has totally relinquished her power. She asked him about her child and accepted his answer like he was God. So what could I do? My mother believed everything he said and he had total control.

This man will make your child believe that this is acceptable behavior and criticize them for not enjoying what they are told is normal. Not to mention he is disciplining your child because you gave him permission. Your child does not feel safe with you anymore and no longer looks at you as their protector. You appear just as helpless as they are. Several times you have forced them to go back to where they are being abused.

64

After awhile I didn't listen to my mother anymore. If my mother told me to stay home and Stephan came over and took me with him, I went. My mama would come home and I would be gone. When my mother saw me she would fuss at me for leaving with him and I'm thinking, "You were going to make go anyway because you always have. Why are you yelling at me?" He took YOUR child out of YOUR house without YOUR permission and YOU told me to do what he says! READERS CAN YOU SEE HOW I WAS CONFUSED!

~~~~~~~

PART 2

O.K. READERS I'M THROUGH WITH MY LESSON FOR NOW, SO LET'S GET DOWN TO THE NITTY GRITTY OF MY STORY!

CHAPTER SIX

My mother finally got a boyfriend. His name was Wendell Sims. He was a chocolate brother with a full beard and mustache. He was well dressed, medium build and he drove a white Cadillac with burgundy interior and it had his initials on the outside doors in the detailing. We didn't know him very well. Except for Stephan, my mother was strict about how we carried ourselves when she had company. We spoke and went back outside or in our rooms. We loved when Wendell came over because my mom was nice and happy and that made us happy. We were allowed to stay outside when the street lights came on. She really loved him and they had a great relationship.

I was 14 years old entering high school and I was happy about that. My sister Gennifer was 18 going into her senior year, Jadon was 16 in the 11th grade and my brother was 12 in the sixth grade. Stephan hadn't been coming around much, but as soon as I entered high school here he comes with his big nose thinking I was going to get a boyfriend or something. He had a new family, her name was Rebi and she was 11 years old. She had 3 younger brothers. Her mother's name was Cynthia. Stephan brought Rebi and her little brother Dwight over to his apartment on Sussex. Dwight was a cute little 6 year old boy with fair skin green/gray/hazel eyes with big pink lips and big ears. Rebi was tall for her age but you could tell she was just a baby. She was an average looking little girl with pigtails and she looked nothing like her little brother. You could tell they had different fathers. Stephan instantly started pitting me and Rebi against each other by comparing us. If I burned a hot dog he would say, "You're so dumb" Rebi got more sense than you and she's only 11." So Rebi and I never got along and Stephan made sure of it. She would lie on me, constantly starting problems and if I said anything back she ran back and told Stephan and put her own twist on it. Stephan would constantly say in front of her that I didn't like her and I was jealous of her. I really didn't have a problem with her because to me, she was just a kid. She started invading my space by stealing my things. When I told Stephan he would say, "You're just being petty! You're trying to get her in trouble because you're jealous of her". He would ask, "Why didn't you put your things up if you knew she would take them?" Stephan was now preoccupied with his new family and always had Rebi with him. But he never strayed too far. He made sure he stayed close enough to monitor what I was doing.

I met Dawn the second semester of my ninth grade year in third period. She invited me over to her house one Saturday and I started to spend a lot of time with her and her family. Dawn was my new best friend. I met her mom and she was such a sweetheart of a lady who instantly made me feel welcome. When Stephan found out he instantly got jealous and started trying to cause trouble by making statements to my mom about how much time I spent over there and making judgments about what kind of girl Dawn probably was. My mom had met Dawn and liked her instantly. She was polite, very smart and from a well mannered family. Her older sisters were already off at college so she was the only one at home. Dawn's parents were divorced but her dad came to see her every day. It was hard for Stephan to start trouble because my mother wasn't hearing him. Stephan would try to start problems with me about how close we were becoming and how much time I spent with her family. I fought back and told him she was my best friend and to get out of my life. Not only did I finally have a friend, I had a mother because Dai made up in areas where my mother lacked. Dai never said a whole lot to me. She was a very quiet lady. It was something about her spirit and aura that always made me feel so comfortable around her. She embraced me as her daughter from day one. To this day she jokes and says, "I fed her one time and haven't been able to get rid of her since!" This was the kind of woman and mother Dai was. All of her daughters had a friend like me that she embraced. Stephan continued to threaten me, saying he was going to tell Dawn I was gay. Usually that made me retreat and end my friendships but this time I told him, "Tell her!" That was the first time I called his bluff. Yes, I thought he was really going to do it. Yes, I thought she was going to stop being my friend but that was a chance I was willing to take because I wasn't giving up my best friend and my new mother. We got in the car and drove over there. Come to find out, Dai and Stephan both grew up in Mobile, Alabama. They lived in the same neighborhood and they knew the same people. Stephan even knew Dawn when she was a kid. Dai said that Stephan was always a strange kid and his family was just as strange. Stephan respected her as his elder so they ended up just talking about the olden days. I had love for Dai because she just made something run smooth in my life where Stephan was concerned, something my mother never did. Now I could be friends with Dawn and I didn't have to worry about him starting problems.

The first time I spent the day with Dawn I rode my sister's boyfriend's bike over to her house. I loved it over there so much that I didn't want to leave so I waited until it was dusk out. I said my goodbyes and rode home. It was getting dark and when I heard a lot of people on this one street, I decided to ride on that street since people were still out. A guy that was about 19, jumped on his bike to catch up with me and tried to ask me out. I politely told him I wasn't interested and I continued on my way. This fool was still following me when I got to my block. I lived four houses from the corner and my end of the block was very quiet because all the kids lived on the other end. When I got to my house I picked up my bike to carry it on the porch and when I sat it down the guy was standing behind me waiting for me to open my door. My inner feelings told me he was waiting for me to open my door so he could push me in and rape me. (Now sometimes criminals need to be careful who they fuck with) I remember thinking, "it aint about to go down like this. Not after all the shit I've been going though." If another man thought he was going to force shit on me he was going to have to kill me! So I turned around and pushed him back with all of my 98lbs which made him stumble back, falling down the stairs but he was quick to recover. He was on his way back up the stairs when I grabbed my bike chain and cracked him on the neck with all my might. I kept swinging until he ran to get back on his bike and got the hell out of there. Do you know he had the nerve to yell back, "BITCH YOU CRAZY!" I hollered back, "YOU DAMN RIGHT I'M CRAZY!" I've been fighting with a grown man since I was 10 and I was not afraid to fight anybody who messed with me! As soon as I got settled in the house; here comes Stephan. You would think he had a GPS on me or something. He started fussing because I was gone all day. He asked me where I had been. I told him, "NONE OF YOUR MUTHA F**KIN' BUSINESS!" He came towards me and I was ready. I had one more ass whooping in me. We had a big dog named

Sebring, a mutt but we loved her and she loved us. She jumped in between me and Stephan growling and barking like crazy. She couldn't stand him either. Sebring planted herself in front of me. I stood there with my arms folded and smirked at him and he backed out the door. Sebring got extra treats for that!

Stephan was very jealous of Dawn. He would try to control me and make me come over and I would say no. He would forbid me to go and say he was on his way to pick me up and I better be there when he got there; I would just say ok. Dawn would pull up and I would leave. One day he had the nerve to come and get me from over Dawn's house. I went out to the car and we had a big argument. He was calling me gay and saying that something must be going on between me and Dawn. BLAH! BLAH! BLAH! So I wouldn't cause any drama over at Dai's, I went back in the house and told Dawn I had to leave. Stephan was right behind me making sure I was going to leave. Dai asked why I was leaving if my mom didn't say I had to. Stephan became very disrespectful. Dai's 5'1" little frame got in his face and let him know that he was not to disrespect her, especially in her house. She told him, "I remember you when you were a snotty nose, dirty little kid. Boy, I changed your diapers." Stephan laughed and apologized because he couldn't believe she just told him off. On the way home whenever he thought about it he started laughing. Even though I left I remember thinking, "she stood up for me!" Years later Dawn told me that night Dai looked at her and said, "He is messing with that baby!" Dawn never told anyone. She was just a kid and didn't have a clue as to what I was going through. She never asked any questions, she would just hug me and say she was sorry.

~~~~~~

Let me explain something to you, I was not gay, fast, or any of the things that Stephan called me. He called me fast when he was convincing my mother I needed watching over. He called me gay when I didn't want to have sex with him or participate in this forced relationship he concocted since I was 7. This was his way of making me feel inadequate. He thought this would make me submit to him and try harder to please him. THAT DIDN'T WORK! Stephan never realized that I was never going to like it or try to like it because I didn't like him. If anyone came into my life that I liked, loved, or cared about; Stephan set out to destroy that relationship by threatening to spread rumors about me.

~~~~~~~~~

In the middle of my 9th grade year, I guess Stephan could predict the future because at 14 I was pregnant. He just left out the part IT WOULD BE BY HIM! I still didn't know anything about sex even though I've been having sex since I was 7. Even though I was pregnant I remember thinking I was still a virgin. When Dawn and I had girl talk and she ask me if I ever had sex I honestly said no and that I've never even had a boyfriend. I didn't know anything about protection, diseases; NOTHING! Stephan told me I was pregnant. I knew that being pregnant meant you were going to have a baby but I was still thinking to myself, "Don't you have to have a boyfriend or a husband for that!" I did notice that I no longer saw the lotion anymore but I thought he ran out.

One day my mom asked me why my stomach was sticking out and I said, "I don't know." I told Stephan she asked about my stomach. I was about 6 weeks. Stephan took me home to tell my mother I was pregnant. I wasn't afraid because I didn't quite comprehended what it meant. My mom was upstairs in her room; when he called her down stairs he went into his act. He pushed me toward her and said, "Tell her!" So I said, "Mama, I'm pregnant." All of a sudden Stephan started yelling, "Sophia she wanted me to do it and I wanted to use something but she wouldn't let me!" EVERYONE PICTURE THIS: STEPHAN PHYSICALLY PICKING ME UP AND THROWNING ME UNDER THE BUS AND EVERY TIRE HITTING ME IN THE HEAD! My mom instantly jumped on me and I was so confused. How was this my fault? You gave me to this man and allowed him to do whatever he wanted to me. REALLY! After everything calmed down my mom sent me downstairs with my sisters and brother. They heard the whole thing and they hugged me and cried with me. When I was called back upstairs I heard my mom telling him to make sure I stayed in school. When Stephan was leaving he told me to come on and I said I wasn't going anywhere with him and called him a two faced dog. Do you know my mother made me go? Maybe my mother didn't know at first but this was a big slap of reality in her face AND SHE MADE ME GO!

The next day when I got home from school, my sisters were there which was unusual because my sisters were very active in sports. Gennifer played basketball, baseball and was offered a full ride to Boston University. Jadon played basketball, baseball, tennis and was a cheerleader. They skipped practice that day because it was time to have an intervention with my mother. They were 17 and 18 years old; they weren't scared of my mother or Stephan. They had it with Mama and Stephan and if that meant my mother wanted to protect that pervert she was going to get fucked up that day. We were sitting around the kitchen table when my mom came in and we told her we wanted to have a family meeting. My mom sat down and my sisters started to tell my mother how Stephan had been molesting them since they were 9 and 11 years old. My eyes bucked because I had no idea. How could we live in the same house and not know we were all being molested? Jadon said he started molesting her the first time he spent the night when we lived on Clement. She said he eased in her bed and woke her up. We all slept in the same room with two sets of bunk beds. Gennifer and Curtis were up top, Jadon and I slept on the bottom bunks while my mother was asleep in her room right next door. You could see the relief on everyone's face when they were able to unburden their shoulders. At this time we finally felt this nightmare was over because my mother could see the whole picture and she could handle this situation. My mother then started by asking. "Why are you just telling me now? What can I do about it now? It was your fault it happened and went on for so long." I said, "Mama it wasn't like we weren't trying to tell you but you believed everything he said." You did everything he told you to do and when Gennifer told you, you slapped her." My mother jumped up and started yelling, "You guys were the ones who liked him and wanted to go with him!" I yelled, "BUT WHO IS THE PARENT?" She started coming towards me blaming me for getting pregnant. My sisters jumped in front of me and told my mother she was not going to put her hands on me over that pervert ever again. It was so quiet you could have heard a pin drop. My oldest sister had a friend that just had an abortion and she got some information from her. They gave my mother the card and told her I wasn't having shit of his and she better take care of it. We all got up and went into our room. My sisters, brother and I slept in the same twin bed that night. We had all just had it! Sure enough two days later I had an abortion. The next time Stephan came over my mother let him have it. She kicked Stephan out of the house and told him not to come around ever again.

2

By the end of the next week Wendell, now my mother's fiancée was shot in the head and killed. My mother was devastated. We all rallied around her in comfort and checked to make sure she was alright. We made sure she didn't need anything and we stayed really quiet so we wouldn't disturb her.

Weird things started happening around the house. The lights would go out for no reason. Detroit Edison would come out and say that someone had pulled the meter out of the sockets in the back of the house. We came home the next day and someone had broken all the basement windows. My two oldest sisters had made their rooms in the basement once they were older in order to have more space.

There was glass all over their bed so my sisters slept upstairs in my room. We all turned in for the night when we heard an explosion. The house instantly became filled with smoke. We yelled to my mother the house was on fire. I ran next door to use the neighbor's phone to call the fire department. While we were watching our house burn, Stephan pulls up and says he heard what happened and he came right over. Now mind you my mother didn't associate with the neighbors and none of them knew Stephan to have his number to even call him. We ended up going to my Aunt Ester's house that night. She lived on the east side of Detroit. We stayed there several days but we had to miss school because she lived so far away. The third night we were there we heard an explosion and my aunt's garage was on fire. The next day Stephan comes to my Aunt's house to talk to my mother. My Aunt Ester couldn't stand Stephan and when he entered her house they went to blows. My aunt grabbed a cast iron skillet and it was on. My aunt had no clue about what he had done to us. She was one of the people who told my mother he was up to something and questioned her on numerous occasions about why he was around us all the time. My mom didn't listen. My mother eventually had to go outside to talk to him because my aunt wouldn't allow him in her house. He told my mom that her fiancé Wendell was into something illegal and they thought my mom knew something. He told her they were after her and her kids because he owed them money. He told her if she stayed over my aunt's house it was putting her in danger. My mother asked how he knew all this. He said; "one night some guys grabbed and blinded folded me and told me to give you the message. They were supposedly contacting you through me because they knew I was your brother". That day we left my aunt's house and moved into one of the flats next door to Stephan's in the shit shack he called home. It was five of us staying in this studio apartment with only a regular size bed in there, so my brother and I slept with my mom. There was a small fold up bed that Jadon slept on and Gennifer slept in a chair with a footstool. We were at his mercy again. We were ordered to come straight home from school and practice because there was somebody after my mother; which put us in danger. The home owners insurance had lapsed on the house because my mother couldn't afford it. If she wanted her house repaired she had to do it herself. My mom was working double time on both jobs. We had no clothes or shoes so we sifted through the rubble and what we found was all we had.

My mother was gone all the time and my sisters had practice after school. I still had to come straight home and be there by myself. Stephan started on me again. I was still bleeding from the abortion and my stomach was always cramped up. I had all these purple bruises on my stomach because with all that was going on and not knowing any better, I had taken a bath. I learned that you are not supposed to take a bath for six weeks after an abortion. At my aunt's house there wasn't a working shower and I got an infection. Stephan ended up taking me to the emergency room and I was sent home with antibiotics. He told my mother that "THE PEOPLE" had poisoned me so I had passed out and he had to carry me to the car. By now we were all home and Stephan is standing in the middle of the floor explaining what was going on; basically letting my mom know because of her involvement with Wendell; she had put her kid's lives in danger. He mentioned in a snarl that she put him out and kept that nigga and now he had to fix what she got herself into. Determined not to let this man get my mom under his thumb again, my sister Jadon told my mother that Stephan pulled that meter off the house. She said, "I had just snuck back in the house and was about to shut the window when I saw him tampering with something on the back of the house and then the lights went off." I told her what the doctor said in the E.R. so she would know I wasn't poisoned. I also told her Stephan made a move on me to have sex that's how he saw my stomach. My mother didn't know what to do. She just knew things were happening around her that set her back financially.

Stephan had convinced my mother that these "PEOPLE" had put something in our system and the treatment we had to take required him to have sex with us. (I AM NOT LYING! I COULDN'T MAKE THIS SHIT UP!) Now this pervert could pick and choose between who he was going to have sex with by saying, "you got treatment today". My oldest sister told him to let her die and she didn't give a fuck! Gennifer had graduated from high school and he was trying to stop her from leaving the box he had us in. Gennifer and Stephan went to blows one day and she stood toe to toe with him and whipped his ass. The next thing I knew, my mother sent my sister away. She was accepted to Boston University and my mother put her on a bus the next day and told her to stay away. I never got to say goodbye to my sister, she was just gone and my mom never told us where. My mother asked Stephan, "Why hasn't anything happened to Gennifer? He claimed he paid the money for them to leave her alone and she didn't need treatment because she was of age, it was just mainly me and Jadon.

My mother was working herself to the bone getting the house back in living condition. Jadon is 18 and she is in her last year of high school. She had a boyfriend named Anthony so Stephan claimed her treatment was over and only I was left. He was really controlling my life now. The only time I saw Dawn was at school but I couldn't stick around to hang out with her because Stephan would be right there at the door when I left school. Every time we wouldn't do as he said something would happen like windows got busted out in the middle of the night or our house would get vandalized and Stephan would say, "Sophia, Toni did this and it caused this to happen and Curtis did that and it caused that to happen" so she would get on us. She was back under his thumb. We did as she said. My mother was dog tired when she got home and the least we could do was not have Stephan come next door with his lies. Every time I was defiant with him, he would get started on how he was putting his life on the line because my mother got into something shady dating Wendell. He started making me responsible for whether or not he continued to keep us alive. He was making me feel obligated again! In so many ways we didn't believe his lies but it would get kind of scary when something happened. My mother believed it so eventually we did too. My mother finally got the house in living condition and we were preparing to move back in our home. The night when she announced that our home passed inspection the house caught on fire again. We were devastated but my mother didn't panic. Stephan didn't know my mom put insurance on the house. This time she didn't have to work like a Hebrew slave and repair the damages herself. Stephan actually did her a favor burning the house down AGAIN! My mother put used furniture in the house so when he burned it down this time everything was covered and got replaced with all new things. We got brand new clothes and shoes. We were back in our brand new house by the end of the month. It didn't make sense to burn it down again because the insurance company would just fix it again and put us up in a hotel.

3

Jadon has graduated from high school and she was on her way to Morgan State University. We started to hear from Gennifer in Boston and she was doing just fine. She even started coming home. She was working midnights at a family living home plus she started a little lawn service where she had regular customers. She also took pictures and sold them as a side hustle. She had bought her first brand new car and we were so excited for her. Jadon didn't do that well at Morgan State because she had a lot of demons she fought every day. She was up and down in weight and would have episodes where she got so angry she would break things so she came back home. Stephan thought he was about to control her life because she had so many issues and mama was stuck on stupid again. Jadon came home one day while Stephan was there and announced that she had joined the Army. She looked at Stephan and my mother with a smirk on her face that said, "Let me see you do something about this, BITCHES!" Once you sign on the dotted line there was no turning back.

~~~~~~~~

My brother had gotten himself in some trouble for a B&E (Breaking and Entering) and he was sent to a youth center so it was just me and my mom there now, which was fine with Stephan because I was who he wanted anyway.

My brother had a couple of friends that lived behind us that stayed in a lot of trouble so they all had juvenile records. My brother wasn't a trouble maker and didn't have a record. Most of the trouble he got into was kid stuff. Now I don't know what possessed him to pull a B&E with those fools but he broke into a neighbor's home that lived two or three houses down from us. They got caught instantly when a neighbor reported to the police that she saw them enter the house from a side window. I remember seeing my brother being led off the side of the house in handcuffs. My mother was at work and as soon as she entered the house I frantically told her what happened and that she needed to go and get Curtis out of jail. My mother went and took a shower. I'm thinking that she was washing the work day off of her and was going to change into something more comfortable before going to see what was going on with my brother. Do you know this heifer went to bed? OOOHHH! I can't stand her.

My mother ignored all the attempts to get her son back. They sent letters to the house, they sent the police, a social worker, they even subpoena her and she refused to go. They eventually sent my brother to a foster home when my mother refused to appear in court to get him out of his situation. My brother was 15 at the time. Now I didn't agree with what my mother did but I have to admit my brother never got in trouble again. Would you if you didn't have anybody who was going to come get you? My mother always said, "Don't go to jail because I will not come to get you." I could have accepted this as a strategy but in my heart I knew the real reason. It was my mother not giving a damn about her children, AGAIN. My mother let my brother get his due punishment for that B&E but she never reprimanded him for putting his hands on the little girls around the neighborhood. He would pick on them for not succumbing to his WHACK advantages or whatever else. He always had a problem with putting his hands on girls.

One day he punched this girl in the eye. For what; I have no idea. She was an only child with no brothers or a father. He never picked with girls who had a male figure in their lives because he wouldn't fight boys. My mother never got on him about that so my sisters and I handled that shit! I saw this girl's eye, it was black and blue, swollen and her eye ball was real red. My eyes watered when I saw her face. I went home and whooped his ass. Since my mother wasn't going to handle it I did. After that if we got wind that he hit any girl, my sisters and I beat him down.

CHAPTER SEVEN

Stephan knew I hated him. I was getting older and it was only so much he could control. I was not listening to him and my mother can kiss my ass. If his information was true about "THE PEOPLE", then she caused this problem and now I had to fuck this pervert to pay her debt. He hung this over my head, WASN'T THAT ABOUT A BITCH! Stephan moved into Cynthia's project apartment on Evergreen and Schoolcraft. She no longer had a boyfriend because she let Stephan run him away like he did everyone's boyfriend. None of these mothers had a man for years. Cynthia's boyfriend Fred told her Stephan shouldn't be trusted and that he was having sex with Rebi. He asked her why Rebi was sleeping with him anyway. When Cynthia asked Stephan, he of course had a reason for her. He said, "Fred wants Rebi. Why else would he be worried about her?" He convinced her that her man was only around to get next to Rebi. When she insulted this man with this, he left. His last words to her were, "you're going to regret this," and SHE DID"! When he left and never called her again Stephan told her, "Oh, that's because I figured out his plan, he knew not to show his face around here again."

Stephan threw my life into another tailspin. This man had been obsessed with me since I was 7! He spent a lot of energy controlling me, keeping me under him, calling what we had a relationship. I'm 17 years old, in my senior year and I'm pregnant. I was hysterical so I ran home and told my mother. This was not my life. I wanted to go off to college like Dawn and the rest of my friends. Stephan tells my mother that I was pregnant because "THE PEOPLE" wanted it and there was nothing we could do about it because I would die if she got me an abortion. Truth is I didn't want an abortion; I didn't want to be a baby killer. It was easier when I was 14 years old because I really didn't understand. As a seventeen year old abortion wasn't what I was about. I JUST DIDN'T WANT TO BE PREGNANT! I settled in with being pregnant because I didn't have a choice. I had to get off the Pommerettes squad at school and enter my senior year pregnant. I remember the night I told Dawn and she cried with me, still not asking any questions. She tried to make me feel better by saying she was excited about being a god mother. I was left with my mother while I was pregnant, especially once I started to show. Stephan stopped having sex with me by then and he wasn't so caught up in keeping up with my whereabouts. WHERE THE HELL WAS I GOING TO GO? He got mad when he knew I was still going over to Dawn's to spend the night and he started in on his shit by telling me Dai wasn't going to let Dawn hang around me anymore when she found out I was pregnant because mothers like her, don't want their daughters hanging around girls like me. (GIRLS LIKE ME, YOU DID THIS, I'M NOT FAST!) They think their daughters will end up pregnant. I tried to hide it for as long as I could. Before I told Dawn I was pregnant, Dai looked at me one day and when I left she said to Dawn, "She's pregnant." I might have been about four months. Dai never judged me, she even came and got me herself after Dawn told her how I had to sit in my room and I didn't even have a T.V. My mother had the nerve to be ashamed of my pregnancy. She didn't talk to me or look at me, she just ignored me. She sent me to the school for pregnant girls at the Castle Building once I started to show. It was alright though, I think I preferred to attend classes there than to be at my regular high school. I didn't want to be stared at and talked about. I remember the day I left school. My mom came up to the school and told my counselor I was pregnant and she wanted to know what my options were. She told her about the Castle Building. I remember my mother explaining to my counselor, without being asked, that she worked nights and that's how I got pregnant without her knowledge. I was told to go and get my things out of my locker. I shared a locker with Dawn. I took all my things out and I left without saying goodbye to my best friend. I was so hurt. I was miserable. I felt all alone. My mother had turned her back on me. My situation was one that she put me in and she turned her back on me! That night I was sitting in my room crying my eyes out because I missed my best friend. I didn't think I was ever going to see her again so Stephan finally won. Then the phone rang and it was Dai she asked me what was wrong and why did I leave school? I told her I was pregnant and my mother enrolled me in the school for pregnant girls. She told me Dawn called her at work crying saying that I left school. She said when she went to the locker all my stuff was gone. She asked me not to leave Dawn and that she has been in her room crying ever since she got home from school. She asked me if I wanted to come over and she came to get me. I remember walking in Dawn's bedroom with her bloodshot eyes and we were so happy to see each other. We sat on the bed and cried. I told her we would always be friends forever and ever AMEN. I finished school because of Dawn. She never said I should but it was because I watched her excel in school. She was so smart. She took her studies very seriously so I took my studies seriously too. I know I finished high school because I didn't want to disappoint Dawn, not that she ever said one word. She was my best friend and she was the only thing in my life that made me happy since I was 7 years old. I finally had someone I was willing to fight for!

2

Wednesday, February 3, 1982 my baby was born, Tiara Kayla. She was 7lbs 5ozs and 19 inches. It was so wild to me because she came out looking like a teddy bear all cute and cuddly. I went to bed the night before and woke up around four am with a strong pain in my stomach it lasted about 3 minutes and I just fell back to sleep. It kept happening more and more for the rest of the night until finally about eight a.m. I went to my mother's room and I told her my stomach was hurting. She told me to call Stephan and get dressed because I was in labor. Stephan showed up by the time I got dressed and took us to the hospital. Stephan yelled at me the whole way saying it was hurting because I was not breathing right. I'm thinking "breathing right" I can't even breathe. My mother stayed very calm and held my hand and told me to squeeze it when I was in pain so she could time my contractions. My mother came into the delivery room with me because Stephan had successfully gotten on my nerves, my mother's nerves, the doctor's and all the nurse's nerves and got put out. I spent two days in the hospital and was released on Friday. When Stephan picked us up he had Dawn in the car. I was so happy to see her. While we were driving home Stephan was on some shit and was mad because I was so happy to see Dawn and I was only talking to her. I was telling her about having a baby and Stephan kept butting in saying, "Having a baby isn't cute. She is going to be a whore or a dike just like you". BLAH! BLAH! BLAH! I started to cry and Dawn just grabbed my hand and shook her head. We dropped Dawn off at home. He took me straight to his house where he lived with Cynthia. All day he hollered about nothing. He screamed about me not knowing what to do with a newborn baby. It was obvious that he was about to hold Tiara over my head to resume control of my life. He had me in his pocket now.

I was back at my regular high school a week later wearing my regular clothes and hanging with Dawn. I would go straight home because Stephan would be there to pick me up. It didn't bother me to go straight home because I wanted to get home to Tiara. Stephan would not let me see her and kept her in the room with Rebi who was now 12 years old. He would make me stay in the room with him. He knew he had full control because my mother told him not to bring the baby to her house. My mother was very ashamed that I had a baby and she didn't want anyone to know. MY SISTERS, BROTHER, MY AUNTS, UNCLES, AND COUSINS DIDN'T EVEN KNOW! Stephan knew how she felt so he took advantage of that. If I wanted to go to the movies with my friends I was trifling and then he would start screaming about who was going to watch Tiara. I had been there all day and to be spiteful, he wouldn't let her come in the room with me. As soon as I wanted to do something then there was no one to watch her. If I wanted to go over to Dawn's house and take her with me, Tiara couldn't go so that meant I couldn't go. As soon as my 6 weeks was up Stephan was on top of me again saying that I still had to get my "sexual treatment" and would call my mother if I put up a fight. The first time he tried it we tore the whole house up. I knocked him down the stairs and he threw a glass at me. We fought for 15 minutes and when we were all tuckered out he took me home and wouldn't let me see Tiara.

It's getting closer to the end of my senior year; prom and graduation was coming up. Do you know this fool thought he was taking me to my prom? He started to come back around when my prom was being planned. When I realized he thought he was taking me to my prom I let him know he was very sadly mistaken. I said, "you're not my man, never been my man and your old ass isn't going nowhere with me." He tried to get my mother to tell me I couldn't go by mentioning what teenagers do on prom night; how much trouble we get into like drinking and drugs. He emphasized how dangerous it was that night because of car accidents but she told him I was going. She told him to leave me alone. She said, "It was bad enough that she still had to deal with you with this so called treatment crap, you got your baby so stop bothering her." Stephan was pissed. I went to prom with my friend Walter who was in my English class with me. I made it home by 12 and Stephan was sitting outside my house when I got there. As soon as I exited the car he jumps out and started accusing me of things. He followed me into the house and woke my mother up. I kept walking toward my room, my mother came down to see what the problem was. Stephan said, "She was damn near fucking in the car and the boy was all over her." My mom informed him that she was waiting up for me and that she saw the car when it pulled up and I got right out. She said, "She didn't even lean over to kiss or hug him good bye!" Stephan started attacking my mother, "You let your kids walk all over you and you will never see Tiara. My mother said, "I don't care and get out of my house." But I cared. My mother wanted me to give my baby to Stephan and move on with my life but that was not going to happen. That was not the mother I wanted to be. I had a responsibility to her and I didn't know what to do but I knew I had to figure it out.

3

Graduation was that Monday and I called Stephan all weekend to see if he was going to bring Tiara to my graduation. He was being a bitch all weekend. Hanging up in my face asking me why I wanted her there. He accused me of wanting to show my baby off. He said I wasn't a mother because all I did was run the street and party, "ummmm, I went to prom." He said 12 year old Rebi was more of a mother than I was. I was very sad and confused at my graduation because I didn't understand how to get a job or how to get my life started. I didn't know anything. My mother was the only person that was at my graduation but Dawn was there to graduate with me. We were in the back touching up our makeup; fixing our hair you know girl stuff. Dawn was standing in front of me pinning my cap on my head and when we turned to look in the mirror to make sure it was straight she looked at me and told me she loved me. I started to cry and she cried with me because she still never understood what was going on with me. She never asked but she still loved me. She always tried to make me feel better. We promised to be best friends forever and ever, AMEN! Even though my mother was the only one there for me when I walked across the stage, Dai and the rest of the Jackson family hooted, hollered and cheered me on. My mom had to work that day so she hugged and kissed me and said she would see me at home. I caught the Grand River bus home even though Dai offered me a ride. I refused because I just wanted to be alone and Dawn was so happy I wanted her to enjoy her day without ruining her joy. I was at my house when Stephan pulled up and got out the car with Tiara. I was very happy to see her but he wouldn't let me hold her. He pretty much let me know if I wanted to see Tiara then I had to be with him so I went in the house, packed my things and moved over to Cynthia's house with him.

Stephan started putting a wedge in between Tiara and I from the beginning. I could be there for days and he wouldn't let me spend any time with her. When I did get to hold her, if she let out the smallest whimper because she was hungry or needed to be changed he would snatch her up and say she didn't like me. He would talk to her in baby talk and say, "What did old bad mommy do to my baby?" He monitored our quality time like a warden. The whole time he would fuss, complain and criticize. When I picked her up he would fuss at me saying I was spoiling her and to put her down. But Rebi was allowed to hold her all day. Over the course of sometime, Tiara started to act scared of me and would shy away from me when I came near her. That broke my heart. She was my baby and I loved her. He purposely kept Tiara away from me so we wouldn't develop a bond. I still feel that distance today. When she was about 16 yrs old I tried to explain to her what I felt the problem was between us. I just started to understand it myself by reading books about how the bond between mother and child was essential at the beginning. I understand now the effect Stephan's actions had on my relationship with my daughter.

Tiara and I have a good relationship. I know she loves me to pieces, she is loyal and always has my back and vise versa. She talks to me about everything. I keep her laughing the whole time on the phone even when she is down. I have the ability to make her feel better when she is going through something. She will say, "I haven't laughed all day, thank you Mommy I feel better" but I still feel that separation between us. Some issues a mother can't fix alone, a child has to be able to filter out nonsense. She is 30 now with her own child. I explained it the best I could once I figured it out and I thought she was able to comprehend this issue. I was the best mother I knew how to be. Through time and her own experiences she will have to mend our tainted bond on her end. Stephan will never win this battle.

Stephan became very verbally and physically abusive when he realized I started backing down when we fought because it was upsetting Tiara. He would push and slap me but I would let it go to end the argument. This went on for a month or so until one day I was standing in the kitchen holding Tiara. We got into an argument because he was showing out in front of Cynthia. I told him about himself, I said, "For me to be all that you're saying I see you always stay in my business. That's why you don't ever have a woman because you have been sniffing my panties since I was 7 years old!" Oh he was heated saying, "I never messed with you when you were a kid. Your Uncle Mark messed with you. You are so in love with me that you confused him with me." My Uncle Mark lived with us for about a month before Stephan came into the picture and he never touched us. He was too busy sneaking grown women in the house to have sex. We could have torn the house up as long as we didn't disturb his groove. I told Stephan, "My Uncle Mark never touched me, it was you. And as far as being in love with you; you have lost your mind. You know I always hated you and still do. So does my sisters and my brother." He picked up a glass and threw it at me. I put my hand up and the glass shattered and cut my hand. If I didn't put my hand up the glass would have hit Tiara in the face. That did it! I walked in the living room handed Tiara to Cynthia, went back in the kitchen and grabbed a butcher knife and said, "you punk ass nigga, you could have hit Tiara with that glass!" The fight was on. He knocked the knife out of my hand so I picked up this stick that was put in the sliding window to keep if from open and started wailing on his ass. He cowered in the corner screaming for me to stop and Cynthia came and grabbed me. I told him if this was going to be my life then I guess we will be fighting because he wasn't going to put his hands on me again.

The next day my mother called and I was totally shocked. She and Stephan got into it because she told him that I had gotten my acceptance letter from Saginaw Valley State College. He said, "Toni is not going to school she has a baby to take care of!" She said, "That's your baby and she's going to school," and she hung up! Stephan called my mother out of her name and criticized me all day saying I was going to flunk out. He said he would fix her. I guess he did too because wouldn't you know I ended up pregnant AGAIN!

The summer was over and time for the college freshman students to be on their way to their new homes, hopefully for the next 4 years. I went over to Dawn's house to watch her pack and even though I was sad that she was leaving I was so happy for her and she was so excited. This is what she talked about the whole 4 years of our friendship. She was going to Clark College in Atlanta, Georgia. I was very proud of her and more proud that she was my friend. She called me the day she was leaving and I felt so sad but she had to go on with her life and I understood that. We promised to be best friends forever and ever, AMEN!

I didn't go to school for another two weeks. I was so conflicted because I wanted to be like everyone else and go off to school but I had a baby and those dreams weren't for me anymore. My mother was determined to get me off to school if it was the last thing she did on this earth. She even came over to Stephan's knocking on the door like the police and told me to get my things and come on. Stephan thought he was about to talk shit but my mother kept walking out to her car. When she took me to school I told her I was pregnant, maybe about 6 weeks and I didn't want an abortion. I told her that I would have to deal with it when the time came but I would make the best of what I had left with my life being in shambles. I went to SVSC for a semester; I came home every weekend to be with Tiara and I did pretty well too. I really enjoyed college life and for the first time, living like a normal teenager. My life was far from normal. I wasn't showing but I was pregnant and I already had a baby at home that needed her mother. When I completed that semester I came home and told my mother I wasn't going back because it wasn't my place to be there. I was a mother and I should be at home with my baby. I'm 18 yrs old now and it was my decision. I had already talked to my counselor and set the ball in motion to finish out my winter semester at home. I was showing now and I had to go back over to Stephan's. I was so miserable over there with all the abuse and the mistreatment. I had no idea how to get out of this box of misery so I accepted this as the rest of my life. I hadn't heard from my sisters or my brother. My mother had turned her back on me. My family still didn't know I had a child and was pregnant with a second. All I had was school, my baby to play with when she was allowed in the room with me and my best friend's letters. Now let me enlighten you about something, Stephan in no means cared anything about me going to college. The only reason I was allowed to go and he made sure I got there; was because he was taking student loans out in my name that I didn't need because I had full financial aid. He claimed that he had to give "THE PEOPLE" this money to pay for the treatment that I now desperately needed because I missed so much being off at school. WHATEVER!

As you notice throughout my whole story I have never mentioned Stephan having a job. HE DIDN'T! NEVER! EVER! He was a con artist; he opened up phony businesses that gave fake references for jobs to apply for credit cards. I later found out that the same crap he was pulling on me with the student loans; he did the same thing to my sisters.

~~~~~~~~~

Jadon told me that Stephan had her apply for a student loan and when she got the money he was bitching all the way to Isle Park saying that he was sorry he got caught up in this mess and it was my mother's fault because she got in a relationship with Wendell who was a criminal. He claimed he was always watching his back trying to keep our family alive and everyone was against him. They made it to Isle Park; his instructions were to put the money in a brown paper bag, tie a brick around it and throw it over the bridge. My sister is not a kid watching a magic show in awe; she saw him do the switch off when he climbed into the car to turn it off. So she asked how they are going to get the money if it was in the water and he replied, "That's what I was instructed to do."

4

Taylor Chanise was born May 18, 1983, 8lbs 11ounces, 21 inches long. She was a little rolly polly and smiled instantly. I was allowed to go back to my mother's house with her but we were not allowed outside. My mother took to Tay a little bit. She would watch her so I could go hang with Dawn when she was home from school. When Stephan found out I was having a little fun when he called for me one day, he was parked outside my house when I got there. I was coming home from hanging with Dawn all day and as I was locking the door, Stephan pushed the door open. He slapped me so now we are having FIGHT #6,893. My mother heard the ruckus and came down stairs with Tay and asked, "What's going on?" Before I could open my mouth he started yelling that I was hanging in the streets like a little whore and I should be at home with my kids. I wasn't a scared little kid intimidated by all that screaming. I told my mother he hit me and he was always putting his hands on me. Stephan and my mother got into it. Stephan was very disrespectful to my mother. I'm now of age and he had control of me through my babies so he no longer had to finesse her. He took Tay and wouldn't let me see her for about a week. Dawn was still here so I spent time with her. When he realized he freed up time for me to have a life, he popped up a week later telling me my kids needed me. When I got there Tay was in her swing screaming her head off. I was told that she had been screaming since Stephan came and got her. Taylor was a momma's baby; she just wanted to be under me so of course when I picked her up she became silent and snuggled in my neck like she had been so abused. We stayed about a week and then Tay and I went back over to my mothers. Several days later Stephan brought Tiara to me and she stayed with me for about two months. Come to find out Stephan had gotten Rebi pregnant at the age of 13 and she miscarried in her fifth month. I thought that little girl looked pregnant but wasn't sure. Rebi was too far along to have an abortion so she had to give birth to the five month old baby that had already died. Her mother was there during the birth of her grandchild and knew that she was pregnant by Stephan. NO SHE DIDN'T CALL THE POLICE OR PUT HIM OUT! He told Cynthia that Rebi was going to be gay and he was counseling her. He said, "I had to have sex with her to get her mind right." Rebi told her mother that Stephan gave her a pill and the next day she miscarried. When Rebi went in for her check up, Stephan stole her file from the doctor's office so they wouldn't have any evidence of Rebi being pregnant and Cynthia watched him do it. Now I know my readers are saying, "You got to be kidding me" but NOPE not at all. This fool had all our mothers drinking the kool aid. By now this little girl was in my predicament. She couldn't go anywhere, had no friends and he was just as preoccupied with her as he was with me when I was that age. He would jump on her and call her out her name.

At 12 years old, little girls have smart mouths. Stephan said something to Rebi one day and she said something smart back. Stephan had a bat in his hand; he hauled off and hit her in her mouth with it. Blood spewed everywhere and her lip instantly swelled up to the size of her head. I just knew when Cynthia got home it was over for him. As soon as she walked in the door Stephan got started, "I had to pop Rebi in her mouth; because Cynthia you know she got a smart ass mouth!" BLAH! BLAH! BLAH! Cynthia understood but I was waiting to see what her reaction would be once she saw her 13 year old daughter's mouth. When she did the house fell silent and Stephan started screaming, "You see what she made me do? Cynthia I'm not going to take your kids mouthing off at me. I do too much for you and them to be treated this way." Cynthia backed down and just said, "Well, she got what she deserved for having a smart ass mouth." WHAT?"

Now I know your mouths are hanging open but Stephan ran his game with Cynthia a little different. Cynthia was working at Wendy's and she worked a lot of hours; all day sometimes. He promised her he could get her a house if she came up with the money. She wasn't home a lot; she left early in the morning and mostly got home about 10 at night. She didn't see her kids much because they were sleep when she left and sleep when she got home. She didn't have a clue what was going on in her household. He had complete control over everything. Cynthia suffered from migraine headaches and had some female problems also. I don't know how and why Stephan had the best drugs but he damn near kept a pharmacy. When she would come in complaining about this pain; Dr. Stephan had the prescription for it and she took it. NO

QUESTIONS ASKED! Cynthia just knew whatever it was, it worked; it got rid of whatever pain was ailing her and she could sleep. After a while Stephan had her strung out on prescription medication. She couldn't get in the house good enough before he was stuffing something down her throat. It got to the point where he was telling her she was in pain and she believed him. When Cynthia did have a day off; she would sleep all day. She was either at work or sleep and everyone was instructed not to wake her so her kids couldn't even see their mother.

Stephan was her pusher and he kept her drugged up. She didn't even know what day it was. He kept her schedule, woke her for work and put her to sleep when she was off. One weekend Stephan drove to Indiana to see his daughter and we were left alone for the weekend. Cynthia and I never had a relationship; we barely knew each other. The only thing she knew about me was the negative things Stephan told her and the only thing I knew about her was the negative things he told me about her but for some reason we liked each other. I don't remember how I ended up sitting on her bed talking till it was light outside but we did. I straightened out a lot of

113

things in her mind. Stephan had her not knowing if she was coming or going. She didn't know if she dreamed she went to work or if she really went work. We started the conversation off very apprehensively because we were not sure if we could trust each other or not. I remember she said, "I think Stephan is drugging me." I said, "He is." I started filling in her blanks for her; things she couldn't remember and things she remembered but wasn't sure if she dreamt them. I told her about my life with Stephan. I explained how I got in my situation and all the bad things he said about her. I also enlightened her that, that wasn't the first time Rebi had been pregnant. He got her 12 year old daughter an abortion right under her nose and hid Rebi in his room. He kept her drugged up and always sleeping so she wouldn't notice.

~~~~~~~~~

One night I was in Stephan's room asleep and I was awakened by Tiara crying in the back room; which was also Rebi's room. I'm wondering why Rebi didn't wake up since she was the one who asked if Tiara could sleep with her that night. Since I was the mother, I got up to get her. It was 3:00 am in the morning; the house is quiet and all you heard is Tiara crying. Stephan is nowhere to be found so I tip toe in Rebi's room to get Tiara. I opened the door slowly not to wake up Rebi since she hadn't gotten up and my mouth drops open. Stephan is having sex with Rebi while my baby is on the other side of the bed crying. I totally lost it! I snatched my baby out the bed and I bust Stephan in his jaw as hard as I could. I cussed Stephan out as I'm walking out of the room. He jumps up with his penis swinging and runs out of the room behind me. This woke up the whole house. Cynthia comes out of her room and the boys are up wondering what the hell is going on. Cynthia is in shock when she comes in the hallway and Stephan is butt naked. That made him realize how this looked. I screamed, "My child is in the room screaming at the top of her lungs and you can't stop to find out what's wrong with her because you were in there having sex with Rebi! Why do you have my baby in the room with you when you could have put her in the room with Taylor and me?" I didn't notice Cynthia standing behind me. He slaps me and tells Cynthia I busted in the room without knocking and that it was disrespectful. I put on my clothes, grabbed my kids and headed out the door. He had the nerve to tell me I wasn't going anywhere but how was he going to stop me, he was still naked. I told him, "FUCK YOU PERVERT!" I started down the street walking with my 1 year old in my arms and my 2 year old in tow. Thank God it was summer because I didn't grab a damn thing. They had on their pajamas and whatever was in the diaper bag when I grabbed it. I walked to the corner store on Evergreen and Fenkell. I made a collect call to Dai and asked her to come and get me. I walked down Fenkell until Dai made it to me. Dai lived at least twenty miles away. Stephan caught up with me at the drug store on Fenkell and Grand River. I went into the drug store with my kids and told the Security guard that I had left their father because he jumped on me and I needed somewhere to wait until my mother got there to pick me up. Stephan came into the drug store but he knew better than to say one word to me. He was afraid of what would come out of my mouth. The traffic was coming in and out of the store and the security guard was standing guard over me. Stephan left back out. Dai pulled up, I got in the car with her and she took me to my mother's house not saying a word and never asking me a question. When she dropped me off she told me to call her if I needed her. Stephan pulls up after Dai made sure we got in the house safely and started knocking on the door. Thank God my mother worked midnights because she surely would have opened the door and made me go back. I ignored his knocks, got the kids ready for bed and went to sleep.

The next morning when my mother got home she realized me and the kids were there. I hadn't seen or talked to my mother in months. You would have thought she would have tried to find out what was wrong or noticed the huge hand print on my face. NOPE! She asked, "What are you doing in my house?" There was a knock on the door and I knew it was Stephan. I looked her in her eyes, took a deep breath, swallowed and asked her could we stay there with her. Stephan was there bright and early to pick me and the kids up. My mother never answered my question. She walked to the door and opened it. That was her response and knowing her embarrassment because of the kids, I knew she wasn't going to let me stay so I walked out of the door with Stephan.

~~~~~~~

Cynthia and I ended up talking the night away. When Stephan got back Cynthia was different and he was confused as hell. Cynthia and I became allies and she wasn't taking anymore of his drugs. She went to the doctor and got her own prescriptions. When she wasn't sure about something she would catch me by myself; she asked me and I told her the truth. Cynthia got another boyfriend named Jason. He worked at Wendy's with her. He was alright looking with a brown complexion, nice hair but was short maybe about 5'5'. Cynthia was a tall woman about 5'10" but that was her boo and Stephan couldn't run him away because he was a little pit bull. Stephan knew not to fuck with him; he didn't even criticize him that was wasted breath.

~~~~~~~

Stephan never did anything for any of these families. He moved into their homes, spent their stamps on their groceries and made sure the kids ate regularly. But like I said ON THEIR STAMPS! He hovered over their aid checks, talked them into getting jobs illegally and he used their money to pay their bills and had the nerve to say, "I do everything for you." Nobody ever thought to say, "You bring no income to this household!" He had sex with all the kids and he called it babysitting.

~~~~~~~

When the summer came my babies and I went back to my mother's house. During my stay at home, my aunt left home with kids in tow because she got tired of her many beatings from her second husband that we didn't know she had. I was standing there in shock thinking, "WHAT HAPPENED TO UNCLE KENNY?" She came over in the middle of the night and that's how she found out I had kids. My mother was so pissed. She treated my aunt; her favorite sister, who helped her whenever she needed it and raised her 1st two children while she worked, like shit! She eventually left and had to go down south to her mother to get away from this man. My Grandma called her abusive husband and told them where they were.

A couple days later after her arrival, her husband pulls up in front of my grandmother's house in Aiken S.C. begging her to come back. She went back of course for more ass whoopings. I was so upset with my mother. I just shook my head, I said, "she going to hell for being such a bitch!" This is not the last time I would think this way about my mother. This is how everyone found out I had babies. My sister Gennifer called me and we cried on the phone. My sister Jadon took it really hard. She said if she had ever had gotten pregnant by Stephan she would have killed herself!

It's September and it's time to go back to school. I was still attending community college but I had to transfer my campus from Greenfield and Joy Road that was right in my neighborhood to the community college campus located downtown. Stephan wouldn't keep Taylor so I could go to school and the downtown campus was the only one with free daycare. Even in the snow, I wrapped my baby up and got on the bus with her. This was Stephan's way of beating me down and making sure I didn't accomplish anything because I told him, "Not another loan was going in my name." My kids didn't have the things they needed because he was using that money on rallying up more kids, buying designer clothes for them and nice gym shoes. I got pissed off because if you recall earlier in the story I told you when we spent the night over on Ilene, there was a girl there named June who was about 14. Well come to find out Stephan had a baby by her at 14 yrs old and her mother Zo allowed it. They moved to Indiana around that time so I never knew what happened to her. He was going back and forth seeing them in Indiana and I think Kristen was about three. One weekend they came here and he took everybody to dinner. Then later took June and their baby shopping and got her everything she needed. My kids were looking like who done it and what for. I had gotten my check from aid and he took my money to wine and dine them; I was heated. That night we had a fight because I told him my babies better get something and quick. He hauled off and slapped me and it was on AGAIN. I'll be damned if he was going to take my money and spend it on his other child! "You better get a job!" He had the nerve to slap me and this was the first time the police got called but it wasn't the last. Stephan tried to mess up my schooling but he didn't because I got my butt on the bus everyday and made it to school on time. Stephan never got the kids anything but by now I'm talking back to my sisters and they would send me money. My sister Gennifer was working for a Children's shoe company in their testing department and they had a program where they actually let kids wear the shoes. The only thing I had to do was when they outgrew the shoes; I had to send them back. My sister hooked my kids up with a closet full of shoes. She would send boxes of shoes and when the time was up I sent them back and she would send more. Stephan tried to start something by saying the shoes hurt their feet and they were messing up their arches "BLAH! BLAH! BLAH!" but we ignored him. Every time Stephan felt like everybody wasn't completely dependent on him and hanging off his every word he would say negative things to get you not to do it. Jadon sent me $20 a week and I would save it and go buy my babies what they needed. Needless to say Stephan had a problem with that. He would say, "If your sisters got it like that then they need to send me some money for your TREATMENT!" WHATEVER! He would ask me constantly did I have any money and I would say, "NOPE!" but the next day my girls would be fresh.

I was 20 years old now and Stephan is still controlling me with this so called TREATMENT. I'm still not sure what that's about. He wasn't too particular about having sex with me because I'm too old but his obsession for me was still there. I was aware of birth control so I was taking my pills like crack. I figure I might not have control over a lot of things but I was in control of having another baby. Stephan didn't want me to go anywhere. I sat in the house all day and night and I played with my babies. They were my playmates. I hated when school was out because I had no other way to get out of the house except when the babies or I had a doctor appointment. I was out of contact with my family again and he totally had me isolated. He knew my mother couldn't say anything (like she ever did) because I was of age. When I didn't obey him, something would happen because "THE PEOPLE" were after us again and it was my fault!

~~~~~~~~

One day Stephan came in mad because Rebi was talking to a little boy that lived next door and she was; what he called, in his face. He and Rebi were arguing into the house and Tiara was crying. He told her to shut up! He whooped Rebi with an extension cord with the excuse to Cynthia that she was outside being fast all up in this boy's face. Tiara kept crying and he popped her on her leg with the extension cord and left a mark. She was two so here we go with FIGHT #7,583! I ran up the stairs and threw my shoulder down like a football player tackling someone and knocked him down. I jumped on top of him and started wailing on him screaming "just because you jealous that Rebi likes someone else don't mean you're going to beat on my baby!" He kicked me in my stomach and got me off of him and when he got up we looked like two bulls waiting to attack each other. He actually knocked the wind out of me but I wasn't going to show it. Dawn was home from school and I told her to come get us. Stephan said I wasn't going but I kept putting the kid's shoes on. When Dawn got there, we left. We got home about 9:00 that night so I could get ready for school. The next day when I came home from school Tiara had been slightly burned from her belly button down to her vagina and as soon as I walked in the house he started yelling, "YOU SEE WHAT YOU DID? YOU DID THIS! NOW THESE PEOPLE ARE HURTING THE KIDS BECAUSE YOUR DUMB ASS WONT LISTEN! THIS IS YOUR FAULT!" I looked down at my baby's bottom half and burst out in tears. He had me for a minute cause I was afraid that something was going to happen to my babies. So I followed his guidelines from then on. Till this day I have no idea how Stephan burned her like that. I imagined some kind of liquid that burned the skin. Stephan was very extreme about keeping me in line as you can tell.

CHAPTER EIGHT

My mother had a friend named Wilson who was about my mother's age, around 37. He had a young girl friend named Kim that was maybe 22. Wilson manipulated her because you could tell she was an air head. She had a 4 yr old daughter named Tracey. I never cared for Wilson too much. He was a woman hating abuser. One day Kim went to my mother and tells her that Stephan had been asking to take Tracey places with him that would require her to spend the night. My mother warned her not to let Tracey go and to stay away from him. Stephan worked his charm on the "dumb in the head" female and she started to sneak and let Tracey go. Then the shit hits the fan because Tracey started complaining about her private parts when her mother gave her baths. They took her to the emergency room and they were informed that she had been penetrated. Wilson whooped off in Kim's behind because Wilson never liked Stephan from the gate. He told Kim that Tracey was not to be around him. My mother gave her advice and she did it anyway. This was the start of Stephan's legal troubles. Kim asked my mother what she should do and she responded, "you do what you are supposed to do and don't take pity on Stephan because he is my brother." Charges were pressed and Stephan went to jail. After his court date he was set free on bond. He goes straight over to my mother's house trying to plead his case telling her that he never touched her, that Wilson was the one who was messing with Tracey and he told Tracey to blame it on him because Wilson didn't like him. My mother told him what she told Kim the day she came seeking advice. He had an attitude but played it off to my mother like he didn't blame her for the advice she gave and that he would have told her the same thing. He thought he could convince my mother to talk to her about dropping the charges.

When Stephan got a chance he tried to contact Kim to plead his case but it caused her to get another butt whooping from Wilson. Tracey wasn't his biological daughter but he was the only daddy that she knew. She was under his protection. Wilson warned Stephan not to call his home again or to have any contact with Kim or Tracey; If he did, his ass was grass.

~~~~~~~

Readers, I know it is probably weird that my mother gave Kim this sound advice but still allowed me to be in my situation with Stephan. I was guilty of this myself. I was babysitting a little girl named Cindy when I was about 12 years old; she was mixed with Indian and black, had long black hair with brownish red skin. She was absolutely beautiful and I loved her. She was about six years old; my job was to pick her up from school and keep her until her mom got home around eight o'clock. Since Stephan required me to be at his house after school, I had to take Cindy home with me. I was very protective of her and I wouldn't allow Stephan to touch her. One day we got into a big argument because he sat her on his lap and I told her to get down and for him to never sit her on his lap again. I explained to him that she was my responsibility and that I wasn't going to let him create any problem for me by touching her inappropriately because her mother would be mad at me. He accused me of calling him a child molester and I said, "You said that. I just said not to put her on your lap any more". I also asked him, "What difference did it make? Why are you stressing so hard to touch her?" He didn't have an answer. He just stormed out of the room. I couldn't protect myself but I wouldn't allow him to touch Cindy. It was like I knew what Stephan was doing was wrong when it came to others but the abuse had been a part of my life for so long I never put myself in the equation.

~~~~~~~

Stephan started with his scheming to get Wilson back. One day Stephan came home and told Cynthia to take Rebi and me to get some Ribs from Style BBQ which is on Hubbell and Fenkell; it would take at least 20 minutes up and 20 minutes back. He also wanted her to stop by the store to pick something up for me but I can't remember what it was. When we got back the house was on fire and the kids were outside. Outside of Rebi, Cynthia had three boys; Travis who was 11, Kiel was 9 and Dwight was about 6 or 7. Cynthia asked them what happened and they told her Stephan made them go upstairs which was unusual, they always stayed down stairs because that is where they slept. They smelled gasoline first because Stephan poured gasoline all over down stairs. Then they heard a window break. Stephan hollered up the stairs for them to get the babies out. YES MY BABIES! Stephan told the boys to say they saw Wilson on the side of the house and that he lit something, threw it in the house and started the fire. They had no idea who Wilson was and had no idea how he looked. But Stephan started hollering at them saying that they did see Wilson start the fire so they started saying what he said. It was a mess because they couldn't keep their lies straight.

We ended up staying at a hotel on Telegraph and Plymouth, living out of the car and buying groceries to cook in their kitchenette. It was summer so no one was in school at the time but the opening of school was coming soon so we had to get settled. Stephan came to us and said he found a house and it was located on Pierson. The house was a nice size ranch home in a very nice neighborhood. Cynthia was very excited because Stephan told her that all THEIR hard work had paid off and HE was able to buy HER a house so we moved in. A month and a half later, Stephan ran in the house and ordered us to pack everything we could carry and get out of the house. He had us squatting and the neighbor reported it to the homeowners. We had to be gone by the time the police got there. We grabbed what we could and left. We ended up living in this one bedroom house on Patton near Plymouth. It was Cynthia, her four kids, me and my two kids and Stephan. We were on top of each other like roaches. Stephan eventually rented him a house around the corner on Evergreen that had four bedrooms. He started living there and we still stayed in the one bedroom. He would come and get me because he had rounded up a new set of kids. I fed them, combed their hair and got them ready for school. My babies were still around the corner so one day I told him to either go get my babies or I was going back around the corner. I wasn't taking care of someone else's kids and my babies were without care.

These little girls and boys ranged from about 6 to about 9. Stephan would walk the neighborhoods and when he found a street full of kids he would join in on their games of two squared, hop scotch, patty cake, buy them all ice cream when the truck came around, meet their parents and the kids loved him. Eventually he would go into his spiel about the kids coming to his house for a movie night with pizza. He would take the whole neighborhood of kids and slowly but surely he would start narrowing it down to the

131

ones he really wanted. He would get closer to their mothers so when he began to take only her kids it just appeared that he was closer to her.

~~~~~~~

Stephan tried to get me in his games of luring little girls into his web when I was about 13 years old. There was a little girl that lived three blocks away from me off of Lyndon and Grand River. I remember she was about eight years old and she always had on really tight shorts that hugged her little butt. For a little girl she had a little fast tail walk on her. I went to school with one of her sisters but I didn't know her personally. At recess, sometimes we would end up competing for first place in double dutch jump rope because we were the last two left but I wasn't going to tell him that. He would watch her and try to make contact with her family in his typical way and when that didn't work he tried to get me to catch her by herself and befriend her. "I'm sorry Stephan but I don't have any 8 year old friends." He actually cussed me out one day because I never tried to make contact with her. I just ignored him and never did what he asked so he dropped it. WHAT A SICK, SICK PERVERT!

~~~~~~

The new kids lived off a street that he visited on one of his random street sweeps. Their names were Tammy and Samantha (Sammy for short) they were two little light skin girls with thick hair that was always neat and they were about 7 and 9. They were typical smart mouth, rolling their eyes little girls. They constantly argued because the older one was always bossing the younger one. I remember going over to the house and Stephan had them watching porn. There were some of his other regulars there like Katie, Patty and a little boy name Carl. These kids came from the new street Carmen moved on called Fielding. I told them to turn that off and they told me that Stephan said they could watch it. I walked over to turn it off and Stephan walks in laughing saying nothing is wrong with it. I rolled my eyes and started to leave; I heard him tell the kids that I had a problem with men and that I liked women but there was nothing wrong with them watching it; it was perfectly normal.

Tammy and Sammy came over often. All the kids loved me because I was nice to them and I was the one who took care of them when they were there. Stephan started to use this to his advantage because all the kids mentioned me and my babies quite often to their mothers. When the mothers asked who I was, Stephan said his wife. "WHAT?" He even started taking my babies with him when he went over there so he would look like a family man and the mothers knew that there was a woman in the house.

2

I told you in the prologue of my story that my oldest daughter who was two at the time told me that her father messed with her in the presence of a little girl named Katie. Stephan gave me a second excuse and tried to convince me that Tiara was talking about Little Stephan (Trent). He actually whooped him like he really did it. He even told Carmen, his mother and she whooped Trent too. He was 11 at this time and the next time I saw Trent he wouldn't look at me because he thought that I believed that he molested Tiara just like the other adults and that I was upset with him. I never believed that Trent wasn't telling the truth. In addition Tiara was very clear who touched her. When Stephan wasn't around I told him to give me a hug and he instantly started crying. I told him that I knew he didn't do what Stephan said he did so just forget about it. He smiled and hugged me tighter. I knew better and before Stephan started in on my babies, one of us had to die. It was ok if I had to be the one to die because I couldn't live with Stephan molesting my babies plus my life was shit thus far anyway. I just knew I wasn't going to lie down like my mother and the others did!

Tammy and Sammy were the nieces of the guys that snatched Stephan out of the house. The girls went home and asked their mother was there anything wrong with watching nasty movies because Stephan allowed them to watch. They told her that he said it was ok but when Toni came over she got mad about it and said that we had no business watching those movies. They told their mother I got mad and went home when Stephan wouldn't turn it off. They wanted to know who was right. Through further investigation they found out that the girls slept in the bed with Stephan with just t-shirts on while he lay in the bed naked. He told them it was ok and that it was no different from what they saw on T.V. He then started touching on the girls and he asked them if they wanted to try what they saw in the movie. He told them that everybody does it and if they did it he would take them to Cedar Point that weekend. He raped those babies that night.

The mother took her children to the emergency room and they said that Tammy (9) had been penetrated but her hymen was not broken. The doctor also said that it looked like someone tried to penetrate Sammy (7) from the bruising down there. The hospital called Protective Services because it is policy to report this sort of crime immediately and they took her babies away.

When their mother got home she contacted the other mothers, informed them what she was told by her children and what happened to her. All the mothers questioned their children but none of them had been touched outside of being fondled. This street was on a witch hunt. The other women called every uncle, brother and nephew they had and they all met up on that block. Tammy and

Sammy's mother called their father and told him what happened. Their dad came over with his brothers. One of the little boys that had been at Stephan's house said, "I can show you were he lives". The girl's daddy looked at his brothers and said, "GO GET HIS ASS!" When the car pulled off, Tammy and Sammy's daddy snatched their mother and beat the living shit out her.

Once they snatched Stephan out his house they took him to the block. They snatched him out the car and when he opened his mouth thinking he was about to finesse his way out of this, he got punched in his mouth. They beat him so bad that somebody finally called the police and that's what saved his life.

I called Cynthia to tell her what happened and while I was on the phone the line clicked, I didn't answer until I got off. The next time the phone rang I picked up. Do you know this fool had the nerve to be talking shit asking me why didn't I pick up the phone? I responded with an attitude saying, "Because I was on it." He started threatening me about what he was going to do to me when he saw me. I sat the phone down and when I picked it back up I said,

"Stephan what do you want because you weren't talking all this shit when you got snatched up out of here." He told me he was in jail and that he needed for me to bring him another shirt. He told me where he was and I took my time getting there. When I finally got to the back where he was, what I saw made my eyes water. Stephan looked like a big headed monster. His left eye was swollen shut with stitches across his eyebrow, his nose was crooked, his lips were so big with stitches in his top lip and he had big swollen knots all over his head. He was almost unrecognizable. His shirt had so much blood on it you would have thought he had on a red t-shirt. Now I knew he had brain damage when he said, "Don't worry about getting me out." I looked at him and said, "Who was worried?"

When Stephan got caught up in this case he still had Tracey's case pending and when he went to jail the second time, they weren't letting him out. When it was time to go to trial the prosecutor opened with all his arrests which weren't many. One accusation stuck out to me, the prosecutor mentioned that he was involved in a situation where he shot a man in the head but was let off on a technicality and it hit me like a ton of bricks, STEPHAN KILLED WENDELL! I started shaking and I really saw the man my mother entrusted me to for all those years. He was a sick, demented, conniving, sexual deviant with serious mental problems. It was mentioned that he was released from the U.S. Army dishonorably for mental instability. Stephan wasn't even his real name. He had three different aliases. REALLY MAMA! I COULD HAVE BEEN DEAD! I SPENT MY WHOLE LIFE FIGHTING A KILLER! Stephan had the audacity to ask his attorney to have me removed from the court room because this was emotionally upsetting for me. He said it like I was his grieving wife. He even tried to hug me like I needed comforting from him. I backed away and screamed, "HELL YEAH I'M UPSET! YOU'RE A FUCKING DEMENTED KILLER! YOU SICK BITCH!" I SNAPPED! I thought I had fainted but I realized I just blanked out. When I snapped out of it, blood was everywhere. Stephan was holding his face in his hands and I was being physically escorted out of the court room by security.

I was put in jail. Actually I got put in what they called a cooling tank because I wouldn't calm down. I was furious. It was a good idea that I calm down first because I hadn't been driving that long and I wasn't in the greatest state of mind. They explained that I was not in jail they just wanted me to calm down. I was in a little cell by myself. I paced and cried. I needed to talk to my mother. I finally sat down and just had myself a good cry. Two hours later they let me out. I went straight home, got my babies fed and off to bed. I took a shower, washed my hair and changed my clothes. I ran straight to my mothers. She wasn't there so I waited on her porch until she got off of work at 11:00. When she got there I told her I had something to tell her. We walked to the store because Stephan had her convinced the house was bugged and they watched her every move. I told her everything I knew.

* I told her about the time when she came home and her bedroom was in disarray. Stephan had me do that. Stephan really wanted me to take her fur coats and put them in the tub and burn them! LESSON FROM LISA "LEFT EYE" LOPEZ, UMMMM NOT A GOOD IDEA! I told her he convinced me to do it because he said if I didn't do it they would burn the house to the ground. I didn't burn her furs but I did tear up her room.

One day on my way to school, I was about in the tenth grade, Stephan picked me up and kept me with him all day till around 7pm. He dropped me off a couple blocks away and told me to act as though somebody had kidnapped me and that I didn't remember a thing with tears, tears and more tears. I did it because once again I was told it would get done for real if I didn't lie about it but they wouldn't let me go. When I got home of course he was there having small talk and even asked me where I had been. I go into my little act and my mom got up and hugged me. I told her that was a lie and I was with Stephan the whole day.

I reminded her of the things my sister told her in the past about seeing him in the back yard the night the lights went out.

I brought to her attention the night of the fire and how quickly Stephan showed up, NOW WHO CALLED HIM!

I told her about how he stroked her ego with compliments but talked about her like a dog behind her back to me, Carmen, Cynthia, and Brenda as well. Do you think she gets the picture by NOW?

I told her everything that had been done to us after my abortion was all Stephan. There were NO PEOPLE! We were never in any danger at least never in any danger from some underworld mafia like Stephan had her thinking all these years. Stephan had a vendetta against my mother when she made me have that abortion. Not because she killed his baby but because she had some nerve making a decision about me. I belonged to him and he did whatever it took to show her that he was in control. Stephan never liked the fact that she thought Wendell was the man! When they started to make plans to get married, Stephan knew he would no longer be able to control her and her children. Once Wendell stepped in, he knew a man was not going to let another man in his woman's life. When he lost control of my mother he also lost access to me. He knew that it wasn't going to be easy to get rid of Wendell like he did everyone else's man because my mother was in love with him. He knew he couldn't say anything to my mother about Wendell and he never wasted his time trying. Then I dropped the BOMB!

I told her that I discovered in court that Stephan killed a man the same way Wendell got killed! He shot a man in the head and got off on a technicality. In case she wasn't getting what I was saying. I said, "Mama, Stephan killed Wendell. I thought my mother was going to pass out. Thank goodness we were just turning the corner to our street. I grabbed my mother around her waist and we held on to each other. We walked the rest of the way home in silence.

3

Stephan called collect a couple of days later and he cussed me out for busting him in his face and opening up the stitches he had in his mouth and over his eye. He informed me that his defense attorney was going to call me and to answer his questions. As soon as we hung up, the phone rang and it was the prosecuting attorney (I knew full well the difference in the two attorneys) but I played dumb and answered all his questions and I offered extra information as well. I kind of snickered a little and Cynthia caught me and this bitch told Stephan the next time he called. He cussed me out and then asked me about the attorney calling and I told him he did. He wanted to know what kind of questions he asked. I told him he asked me did I ever see him touch any of the kids. I told him I answered, "No." (Information I volunteered: But I wasn't in the room with them and he would lock the door!) Did the kids sleep in the bed with him? "YES". Was it all of them at the same time or one at a time? I answered, "One at a time". When Stephan heard the line of questioning he asked, "Who was this person you talk to?" I told him his name. Stephan realized I talked to the prosecuting attorney and he was livid. I said, "You told me to answer his questions honestly."

It was one particular little girl named Katie that was over when this situation happened. He told me not to take her home to keep her there with me. The shit was all over the news and her parents were calling for her. The mother didn't even know where Stephan lived to send the police. Who lets their child go somewhere and they don't know where the person lives? Katie was about 11 and she had no idea what was going on. Stephan called me and said, "Don't take her home until I tell you." When we hung up I told Katie to come here. I gave her a hug, grabbed her things and took her home. The next day when he called I told Stephan I took her home and he started cussing and I hung up. He called back and Cynthia answered but by then I was out the door. He tried to stay calm with me because even though he kept me ignorant he knew I was smart and I was the only outside connection he had so he played nice. He said, "It wasn't your fault you talked to the wrong attorney because I should have been clear. He said he wasn't mad about me taking Katie home because he knew that I thought it was the right thing to do. Uh Huh! Stephan was sentenced to 18 months to 10 years at Jackson Prison.

I know you are thinking, "YOUR'RE FREE, YOU'RE FREE! THANK GOD YOU ARE FREE! NOT! I did all those things preparing to die. If these so called "PEOPLE" really exist then I would be on their shit list or in Stephan's words "he was the reason we were alive and without him we lose our protection". I was still in the mental and emotional prison that he had sentenced me to since I was 7 yrs old. I was afraid and confused. I didn't know how to do anything and he made sure of it. That was part of his control. I remember living my life thinking that I was going to be kidnapped and tortured by these "PEOPLE". I would think, "Well, I might as well go to school until they kill us or I might as well get a job until they kill us."

CHAPTER NINE

Stephan was sent to Jackson Prison and after his quarantine period (30 days) he began to call the house to give us directions about the things he needed us to do. That went on for several months. One day Stephan called and he was talking about getting money sent to him and keeping his books full. All the money we had coming in just took care of the bills. Now hold on to your seat because this fool surely had lost it! He had the nerve to ask; no insist that I find a man that would give me money and then I could send it to him. I remembered thinking, "THIS FOOL HAS LOST HIS MIND IF HE THINKS HE WAS GOING TO PIMP ME FROM PRISON!" I remained very calm and just listened to him tell me there was nothing wrong with it and I should sleep with him because he would do anything for me after that. REALLY STEPHAN! I MEAN REALLY! I started planning my exit right then and there. I didn't know what I was going to do or how to do it but I surely was going to find out.

I told Stephan the next time he called that I was looking for a job and he forbade me to get a job because he wanted me to be able to come see him on the regular. I remained calm and just listened because I already knew what I was going to do and that was GET A JOB! Cynthia got me a job at Wendy's and the next time Stephan called I was at work. He couldn't say much but he threatened me. He told me that I better come up to Jackson whenever he told me. It took a minute to get me on his list so I just worked. He would call everyday to tell me how he wanted me to pay the bills and anything else he wanted me to do. When he talked to me over the phone he would talk very disrespectful so the guys in line could hear him dog me and they would laugh. OH, FOR REAL! OK! I was in charge of the house and Cynthia didn't mind because she wasn't good with bills so I paid the bills, bought the groceries and anything else that had to be done to maintain a household.

Rebi had a smart ass mouth with her mother but she didn't know what to do with me. She was about 16 yrs old and was tall like her mother. I made it real clear that her ass was going to fall in line. One day she was in a funk because the last couple of times Stephan called he just talked to me and hung up. She went in my closet and cut up all my clothes because I dressed really nice when I went to school. My sisters made sure my kids and I had at least the things we needed. They were still sending me money. I came home from work and I noticed my closet door was open and I immediately knew that Rebi was in my things. I noticed how my clothes were hanging awkwardly and when I checked my clothes they had all been sliced up but Rebi wasn't home. I called Cynthia over her boyfriend's house and told her what she did and Cynthia said, "Oh well. Handle that as you will." Rebi was getting beside herself. She was disrespecting Cynthia, bullying her brothers, skipping school and entertaining boys at all hours of the night. I didn't trip because she was Cynthia's problem. I went in the kitchen to clean my babies up. Tiara wasn't feeling well, she was burning up. I picked her up to check her out. I looked at her face and she had marks and scratches on her face like she was hit in the face with a switch. I asked her what happened to her face and she said, "Rebi hit me in the face with a stick." WHAT! I asked, "Why?" Tiara said, "Because I was crying." I put Tiara clothes on and took her to E.R. Being a young, inexperienced mother I didn't know what was in store for me when I decided to take my baby to the E.R. with a mark on her face. They asked me what happened to her face and I told them the kids were playing with switches like they were swords and she walked right into one. That was the end of that so I thought. I had been sitting back in the E.R. for hours and when the doctors came back they had security with them and Protective Services. They explained to me that they were going to take Tiara until they investigated this situation. Tiara grabbed hold to me and told them that Rebi hit her in the face and that mommy didn't do it. Now I didn't know a lot but I knew not to let them take my baby and put her in the system; it would be too hard to get her back. So me and Tiara held onto each other and wouldn't let go. I cried, pleaded and begged for hours. Tiara was crying saying I didn't hit her, Tiara was treated for an ear infection and her fever. They eventually allowed me to take her home with an investigation pending.

I finally got home and I was exhausted. Cynthia was up getting the kids ready for school and she was getting ready for work. She asked, "What took so long?" I told her the whole story and she gasped at Tiara's face. When she approached Rebi about it THAT BITCH GOT SMART! I couldn't tell you what she said because I didn't let her get it out. I punched her dead in her mouth and the fight was on. I fell back on the couch and she was on top of me. I took my foot and kicked her off of me which made her fall back against the wall and that was all I needed. I got to my feet and started wailing on her ass until Cynthia and her sons came and got me off of her which took a minute. She grabbed me by my waist and pulled me but I got one good kick off in her nose and blood gushed everywhere. She had a black eye and a busted nose.

4

I called my mother and told her that I needed help and I asked her could I come home and she said "yes". I started packing my things; Cynthia was very upset and begged me not to go. I gave her a hug and told her I loved her but I needed to start my life. I didn't know what I was going to do but I had to find my way. That day I was scheduled to go see Stephan. I got the kids situated and loaded them in my car; I had brought a 79 Maverick. While there, Stephan went to put Tiara on his lap and I snatched her off and told her to sit on her own butt. I stared at him like everyone in here will know why you are here if you want to front on me. He was quiet and needed me; he wanted me to take Cynthia's bill money and send it to him with instructions not to tell her. I sat quite and listened.

~~~~~~~

On my way home my car threw a rod. My babies and I were stranded on the side of the freeway all night. It was winter time and we had no heat. I crawled in the back seat with my babies and we cuddled together to stay warm. When it was day break this really nice lady stopped and gave us a ride to the next rest area and gave me money to call my mom. THANK GOD FOR GOOD SAMARITANS! I was stranded in a city called Chelsea, Michigan. I had a coworker that had a little crush on me. We would sit in the dining room and eat lunch together. I called him and he came and got us. I was moving that day and didn't have enough stuff to fill a truck but I had to rent the truck with the hitch to get my car back home. I hadn't been driving long enough to drive a U-Haul truck with a hitch attached but I didn't have a choice. The man at U-Haul gave me a quick lesson on how to hook my car up once I got to my car. I loaded my babies in the truck and we were back on the road. I forgot some of the instructions that he told me but the directions were on the side of the truck. I made it back home and parked my car in front of my mom's house and I used the truck to get my things from Cynthia's. When she got home I was gone. When I got to work the next day, I told Cynthia that Stephan wanted me to keep taking her money but instead of paying her bills he wanted me to send the money to him. I told her if she wanted me to keep her bills paid I would do that because she was so scared of this responsibility; she thanked me. The next time Stephan called I told him Cynthia said she was going to pay her bills herself and she conveniently was never home when he called.

CHAPTER TEN

I'm back at home with my mother and Stephan is calling my mother's house trying to get me to come see him. I was working long hours and had become a team leader so I was making a little bit more money. He tried to run that crap on me that we were still in danger. We had to pay "THE PEOPLE" their money. I told him I didn't have it. I needed to take care of my babies so he would get NOTHING! He still was showing out on the phone because somewhere in his fucked up mind he thought he was going to control me from prison. He went on one of his tyrants and said, "I WANT YOUR ASS UP HERE TOMORROW AND BITCH………. CLICK; I hung up! He called back a couple thousand times and I eventually unplugged the phones throughout the house. My mother didn't know because she was not a phone person anyway and her phone rarely rang. A couple of days later when I plugged the phone up to make a call it started to ring; I didn't answer it. I waited until it stopped ringing and then placed my call. The next time it rang I answered it, when the operator went into her little spiel about accepting the call I said "NO!"

My mother and I didn't have much to say to each other. I was grateful she let me come home but I knew she didn't want us there. She kept my babies for me while I went to work but that was it. When I walked in the house she handed them right over like she was punching a clock. The peace didn't last long; my mother was never a grandmother to my children. She had her ass on her shoulders like this shit wasn't her fault. She blamed me. She despised me for wanting and loving my babies. I never looked at my babies and saw Stephan; my oldest daughter looks just like him and she is beautiful. They were my babies and I loved them. They were my best friends and they needed me if they were going to have a chance. They were my responsibility.

One day I came home from work and I was dog tired and my babies were already in the bed asleep. I went to kiss them and Tiara woke up and she had a BIG ASS HAND PRINT ON HER FACE! I asked her what happened to her face and she said, "Grandmommy slapped me." My baby was 3 yrs old and she had a hand print on her face. Now Readers, I knew my mother was a BITCH! I knew she would put us out in the middle of the night but that was going to have to happen because I would be damned if she was going to put her hands on my babies and I didn't say something about it. She has never supported me nor has she acted as a grandmother. I took three steps at a time; I never disrespected my mother before even after all the shit she let me go through but this wasn't about mother and daughter, this was about mother to mother. My mother knew me well, she knew that I was about to be in her face and she was waiting in the kitchen for me. I said very calmly, "Tiara said you hit her in face. What did she do to deserve that? She is only 3?" My mother in her usual calm voice told me that she didn't have to explain anything; she hit her because she hit her! I totally lost it. I let her know that she was never to put her hands on my babies again and since she was so big and bad why didn't she use that attitude with Stephan when he was fucking all her daughters. She told me that I could take those things and get out of her house. I told her I wasn't going anywhere and that she owed me! I walked back to my babies and got in the bed with them and cried. My babies wrapped their arms around me and we fell asleep! The next day I enrolled my babies in daycare. I had no idea how I was going to pay for it.

2

It was the month of December and my sister Jadon was coming home. She just had my little nephew Phillip and I was so excited to know I was an auntie. When I heard the knock on the door I jumped up to answer it, my mother stopped me and answered the door herself. She opened the door and kept her arm in the way so my sister couldn't get in. My mother asked her what she wanted. WHAT? My sister had not been home for years. I haven't seen her but I talked to her on the phone so I was excited to see her and my new nephew. I said, "what do you mean what does she want, she's here to see me." My mother looked down at her grandchild never taking the cover off to look at him. Jadon was still standing outside in the cold with snow up to her knees because we had a bad snow storm earlier that day. My mother said, "That thing is not allowed in my house." My sister turned around and walked away. I was livid! Once again I'm about to get put out! "Mama, have you lost your ever loving mind. How are you going to turn your daughter and your grandchild away in a blizzard? This is why all your kids hate you now! You have never had our back and you are never there for us!"

My mother turned and walked back upstairs. My mother thought my sister was coming home to ask to stay with her now that she had a baby. My sister joined the army when she was 19 yrs old and was coming home to get the rest of her things because they were sending her to Germany. Years later my sister lost her son to his father's side of the family. When you are in the service, if you get a tour of duty and you have a baby, you have to give someone temporary custody of your child. My sister has known this family throughout high school. Anthony was her high school sweetheart and they welcomed her with open arms. She loved them and she thought they loved her. She trusted them and gave them temporary custody of Phillip. When she got back from Germany she walked straight into a court battle. She was in South Carolina and when she walked into the court room, Anthony and his whole family had flown to South Carolina TO PROVE HER UNFIT. She lost Phillip to them for lack of family support and she had to pay Anthony child support. Anthony was in the marines and wasn't there either. He never raised Phillip a day in his life. My mother lived 5 blocks away from the Ratz family and she never went to get him or to see him. COLD HEARTED BITCH!

3

Stephan continued to call me and after getting no response he wrote me a letter saying he was sorry and that he knew he had really done me wrong over the years. He admitted getting me pregnant on purpose to hold onto me because I was young and he knew I didn't care about a relationship with him (there he goes with that word again) he knew he would lose me once I graduated from high school. He begged me to please come to visit him and that if I could find it in my heart would I send him money every once in a while if I had it. NEVER DID EITHER ONE!

I never responded to his letter so he turned back to the nasty, manipulative, conniving asshole I was accustomed to. He reported me to Social Services and told them I was working. I got kicked off aid. He called my job and told them that I was a mule for a big time drug dealer and transported drugs back and forth from city to city and that I would be ruthless enough to sell it at work. That didn't work because my manager had become a very good friend and I had confided in her about my past. He even had the FBI at my mother's house saying that I was selling drugs there. We weren't there when they came by. My neighbor told me they questioned her about me and that blew over.

Stephan continuously called. I didn't accept any calls or return any letters. He even had Cynthia come over with messages of threats; we laughed. She only told me because she knew I would get a big kick out of it. He even got her kicked off of aid because she stopped taking his calls. He was running up her phone bill having her make calls for him that sometime took hours. She was tired of his bitching too.

THE ULTIMUM BETRAYAL

I remember coming home from work and I went down stairs to see my babies and they weren't there. I figured they were upstairs with my mother. When I got upstairs my mother was in the kitchen and I asked, "Where are my babies?" She said that Stephan called and told her that he had somebody coming by to pick

161

them up and to pack all their things. Some lady came to the door and she gave my babies to her. MY MOTHER GAVE MY BABIES AWAY! When I asked her who she was, she said, "I didn't ask!" It felt like somebody had snatched my insides out. My mother said, "I don't know why you want those kids anyway. You don't need them." I did need them and they needed me. I cried for hours because I didn't have a clue where to start to look for them. Stephan got his wish. I had to see him. I called my sister in Boston and told her what Mama did to me and that I had to see Stephan but I didn't have a way because my car was still down. I'd been catching a bus for over a year. My sister jumped in her car and drove through the night and made it to Detroit by morning. She had no words for my mother when she got there. She just looked at her, put her head down and shook her head and we walked out the door. When we made it to Jackson Prison do you know this fool had the nerve to come out with a smile like this was a regular visit? Acting as though my sister was there to visit him, he went to hug my sister and she pushed him away by his face and I sat down. He tried to make small talk but Gennifer cut straight to the chase and said, "just tell my sister where her children are." He didn't give me the information until the end of the visit. I played nice to make him think we were all good knowing I would never visit him again.

CHAPTER ELEVEN

My babies had been picked up by a woman named Ma Bea, she was a minister. I have known her my whole life. As soon as we got off the road I went straight to Ma Bea's house to see my babies. Stephan left her strict instructions that I was not allowed to take the kids with me. He told her all types of lies, that I was physically abusing my babies, I stayed in the street and I was neglecting them. She was very apprehensive when I came to her house and she didn't know what to think so she honored what he said. I had a lot of respect for Ma Bea. I didn't put up a fuss and plus my kids were safe so I left them there. She watched my every move when I would visit and she would not let them out of her sight. I wasn't allowed to take them anywhere. If I wanted to see them I had to see them at her house; I practically moved in. I wouldn't go home to my mother's house until late at night. I went to see them every day when I got off of work at 3:00. I stayed there until bedtime. I combed their hair, gave them their baths and lay with them until they fell asleep. After a while she let me spend the weekend with her because I didn't work on the weekends. They were with Ma Bea for about eight months and I pretty much lived there, I just didn't sleep there. I helped Ma Bea cook and clean, went to the grocery store for her or anything else she needed. I loved Ma Bea and I really appreciated her because she was very nice to me and she always has been even when I was a little girl.

Ma Bea owned a store with a two family flat in the back. Her son and his wife lived back there and ran the store for her. Ma Bea and Ms. Raine ended up being the angels that came in my life. Ms. Raine was barren so when Ma Bea brought Tiara and Taylor to the store she thought they were the best thing since sliced bread. The first thing she asked was, "where did they come from?" Ma Bea explained and she was so happy. She asked Ma Bea, "Can we have them? Can we keep them?" The first time she met me she welcomed me with open arms and thanked me for sharing my babies with her.

Stephan was back to his shanignans again. He was mad because after I found the location of my babies I refused to communicate with him AT ALL! I completely faded to black on him. He would call over to Ma Bea's and I would refuse to answer the phone. He was getting on her nerves with all his bitching and complaining. He was always putting me down trying to tell her I was this awful person. He didn't know I was spending so much time with her and that she was getting to know me for herself. She was able to see through all his lies. The hanging out Stephan claimed I was doing, she knew I wasn't doing. She would tell Stephan, "This chile doesn't even have any friends so what are you talking about?" Sometimes she would get so frustrated that she would say, "Stephan just call for your kids and leave this chile alone!"

She really had it with him the day he called and told her he wanted her to call protective service on me for abandonment. He got nasty with her when she refused to do it. She had a conversation with Ms.Raine about it the first time he said it; neither agreed with his criticism of my parenting skills. Ms.Raine told her that she didn't trust him or like him. She would say my babies were too well mannered and too well taken care of for me not to love them. When we lived with my mother, every Sunday I washed all their clothes, ironed them, shampooed and French braided their hair w/ beads. It just made it easier to get them ready every morning for daycare so I could get to work on time. Every Wednesday I took their hair down and rebraided it with the beads. That Monday when she picked them up without my permission; all my mother had to do was put their freshly washed, pressed, and folded clothes in their little duffle bag with their barrette bucket. Ma Bea told me that confused her from the beginning because it wasn't like I knew she was coming to get them.

Eventually, Ma Bea allowed me to take them away from the house. She even let them start spending the night with me and she let me keep them for days. They started spending time with Ms. Raine and staying at the store with her. Ma Bea was about 70 years old and she didn't have the energy to really care for these active 2 and 3 year old children. I was always there and Ms. Raine let them stay at the store with her while Ma Bea made her rounds to her congregation and other things she was responsible for as a minister.

When Ma Bea refused to call Protective Service, Stephan called them himself and they showed up on her porch one day. That did it for her. That day when I came over to visit, she had all their things packed up and she told me that she trusted me as a mother and she thought I was doing a great job. She apologized for being suspicious of me but she didn't know what to think after what Stephan told her about me. She knew me for herself now and she knew Stephan was using her to keep a hold on me. She knew that I had my priorities right and she trusted me to do right by them. She told me she was doing what she was doing because she refused to take part in Stephan's plot to control me. She was always suspicious of Stephan's wrong doing to me when I was a child and for me to have children by him confirmed it. She told me that I had aged beyond my years; that I had a lot more maturity then girls my age because I had been through so much. She said that I had a glow about me, a light that would touch others just by me being in their presence. She apologized to me for not coming to my rescue sooner but she could do something now. Ma Bea prayed over me that day; she asked God to watch over me and to guide me. She told me not to be afraid because everything that I needed to survive, I already held it inside of me and to walk in faith. That day she released me from

Stephan's control, she was the last connection that he had to me!

NOW I WAS FREE!!!!!!!!!!

CHAPTER TWELVE

Haunted Past

I never personally heard from Stephan again or laid eyes on him. However, my past has come back to haunt me several times. Some years ago I had a friend who had an uncle in Jackson Prison and she asked me to go with her to visit him. Her uncle had a friend that never got any visitors and he asked me to call him out since there were two of us. All four of us took a picture together before we left. A couple of weeks later my friend received a letter at her home for me from one of the little boys that lived in my nightmare and was also sexually abused by Stephan, named Trent. We wrote letters back and forth for a while and in these letters he told me about his nightmare of sexual abuse by Stephan. He said Stephan use to make Trent (5) and Sweetie (4), have sex and laughed. Trent told me that Stephan would only have oral sex with him. He also told me that his mother blamed me for what happened to him and she promised if she ever saw me she would beat my ass because I was in cahoots with Stephan. "WHAT?" I WAS A CHILD, WHY DIDN'T SHE HELP ME! I was 11 years old when I met Carmen and she didn't think it was strange for me to be in a studio apartment with one bed with a grown man? She didn't think there was something wrong when she came upstairs and I was lying in the bed with no clothes on? How about just having life experience? She didn't feel anything was wrong with the whole picture? After I read that letter I put my shoes on and drove over to Fielding Street off of Seven mile to meet the bitch half way. I couldn't remember the house because it had been so many years since I had been over there. I guess it wasn't the day for me to go to jail.

He told me that my brother was also sexually abused by Stephan. I never knew that Stephan molested little boys. I thought I knew and had seen everything since I was there from the beginning. When I found that out, I was totally broken. Once again I thought to myself, we all lived in the same house, we were all being sexually abused and we did not know about each other. Trent reminded me about the gun shot hole in the wall over at the Sussex dump.

What happened was my brother was getting up in age and Stephan thought he was going to continue to punk my brother and Curtis had enough. Stephan tried his usual little spiel and thought he was going to force my brother into having sex with him. Curtis grabbed his shot gun and tried to blow his head off. I think he was 13 years old at the time. That was the last time Stephan tried anything with Curtis. I called my brother out in California and asked him about it and he said it was true. I asked him did Mama know he said, "Yes." I asked, "What did she say?" He said, "She called me a punk and said it was my fault because I was a man and I should have defended myself." Uhg! If I was seven, Curtis was five! HELLO! My brother and I cried together on the phone that day and I told him I was sorry. He said, "I really felt the sorriest for you. You got the worst of our situation." TEARS.

2

One night I was at a cabaret and was standing near the dance floor; a guy came over to me and said his friend wanted to talk to me. I asked, "Why can't he come over here?" (with my face all torn up) and I said I wasn't coming. He walked back over to his friend and ten minutes later the guy came back. He was very hostile and he asked me if I was going to come over and I said, "NO!" He stood there and I said, "WHAT YOU'RE GOING TO HIT ME BECAUSE I WON'T GO TALK TO YOUR FRIEND!" He started to walk away but stopped and said, "Oh, you can't come over to talk to the man who slit the nigga's throat that molested you your whole life!" That got my feet moving; who was this person? As I walked over to him he had on a hat with a trench coat and he looked like a dark shadow. I had to get right up on him to see who he was and I gasped! It was Mannie, Trent's brother. He grabbed me and hugged me. He told me he was so happy to see me. He said he always wondered how I was doing and he prayed that I was alright. We stood and talked for a minute. He told me he always knew what

Stephan was doing to me. He told his mother time and time again to stay away from him. He also told me that his mother blamed me for what happened. They stayed into it because he always argued the point that I was a child and she should have known better. He argued with his mother for criticizing me. He told her he would never forgive her for not protecting his little brother. I told him I feared that one day I would be out with my babies and run into Stephan. He would try to get my babies away from me. I told him I was afraid that I wouldn't be able to hold onto both of them. He assured me that he was not a problem anymore and to go ahead and live my life without being afraid. He told me he always kept up with Stephan's whereabouts throughout his life. Freaky right! I left the club right after that conversation and I felt a sigh of relief that the devil finally got his due! I called everybody that was a part of my nightmare and let them know of the information I received that night. Years later with the technology age we live in, my daughter Taylor still gets a kick out of running names through the system to see what information she can retrieve. She found that Stephan wasn't dead. He is serving a life sentence in jail for abduction and child molestation. I believe Mannie did what he said he did. He really hated Stephan and I'm sure if they ever cross paths he wouldn't hesitate to punish him but God chose for Stephan to finish out his life of hell in prison before he is banished to eternal damnation.

3

I was walking in a store about 3 years ago and ran into an old friend from my neighborhood and she asked, "Whatever happened to that weird guy that hung around your family?" She expressed her dislike for Stephan and told me about them getting into it. I knew nothing about this situation. She said she went to pick up her son from school and stopped at his classroom door but she didn't see him so she drove to find a parking space. That's when she saw Stephan putting her son into his car. She jumped out of her car, ran and grabbed her son and asked him, "WHERE THE FUCK ARE YOU TAKING MY SON!" He told her that he was there picking up his son and saw her son and was going to bring him home for her. She slapped the shit out of him and started walking towards her car as she beat her son for going with him. She got a glimpse of his back seat and saw tape, rope and kid's toys back there and that's when she

started screaming for the police. . . . .

4

When Stephan had Ma Bea come and get my babies, I lost touch with Cynthia for about a year. I was living on Prevost off of Joy Road and I bumped into her oldest son at a store around the corner from where I lived; I was so glad to see him. He told me that shortly after I moved out Cynthia moved in with her mother on Stopel. I surprised her one day and stopped by to see how she was doing. My greeting was not what I expected because I thought we had become such good friends. She was very dry but I was so excited to see her. We were sitting down talking in the living room when Jason came into the room. I was surprised to see that they were still together after all this time so I embraced him as well. I got up to greet him and he pushed me away. He started fussing about how I stole Cynthia's money and that I was sending it to that nigga. I was shocked to hear him say that because I paid Cynthia's bill every time she gave me her bill money and I gave her the receipts. I also had my own copies just in case something happened we could prove we paid the bill. I also did it because I knew Cynthia wasn't the best record keeper and she probably would lose hers or wouldn't keep them together. (That bill had to be paid because it was done on some illegal crap Stephan pulled so to keep any heat off of her we paid it.) I asked Cynthia, "What is he talking about?" I said, "Cynthia you know I paid every bill and gave you the receipt." She looked at me with guilty eyes and said nothing. Jason started hollering at her saying to stick up for herself and stop being so scary. Jason said, "Cynthia didn't you tell me that your shit was fucked up because you were giving Toni all your money to pay your bills and you found out she wasn't paying them and was sending the money to Stephan? Ain't that why we had to come and live with your mother?" I was shocked. I said, "All what money, I was paying one bill for $120.00 but her household bills were on her. She jumped up and called me a liar. Jason accused me of being in on Stephan's kiddy rape and punched me in the face. I had my first black eye. I was so hurt that she called me a liar and a thief that I didn't even react when Jason hit me. I just stared at her. She couldn't even look me in the face. I turned and walked out the door. Once again I was accused of Stephan's sins. I was just a kid who was also being molested by him.

I went home and went through my files because I never threw receipts away. I found all my copies very easily. I jumped in my car headed to Cynthia's to prove my innocence. I turned around and decided not to go because I didn't have to prove anything to Jason. Cynthia knew I paid that bill that's why she couldn't look at me. I threw the receipts in my glove compartment.

That hurt me so bad because I was the one who went through hell. No one had it worse than me. To be accused of being a part of his sickness was unbearable. I too was one of his victims. I was just older than the others but still I was just a kid. The mothers were my mother, Cynthia, Carmen and Brenda. They blamed me for their irresponsibility and neglect. They all felt like a bunch of fools and they were so I guess they had to blame somebody to ease their conscience.

Several weeks later I ran into Cynthia's oldest son in the neighborhood again. He gave me a hug and said he was sorry for what happened. He walked me to my car and I said, "I have something for your mother" and handed him all the receipts to his mother's bills. He told me that I didn't have to prove anything to him or his mother. She told him that she lied on me because she hadn't been paying the bills and Jason kept asking her what was happening to the bill money. She told him that to get him off her back. She didn't think she would ever see me again so she thought it was safe to blame me. That just pissed me off. I gave him a hug and told him to take care of himself and before I could get in the car he said, "Toni, my mother is strung out on that shit. She started smoking crack a couple of months after you left." TEARS.

~~~~~~

5

My daughter moved to Southfield after my first grandson was born. One day we were going through the security gates and I recognized the security guard. It was Brenda, Sweetie's mother. We were so happy to see each other. I hadn't seen her since I was 17 years old. We stood there playing catch up and I showed her pictures of my babies and when I showed her a picture of Tiara she turned green like she wanted to throw up and said, "I can't look at your daughter, she looks just like Stephan!" Taylor instantly got an attitude and said, "But she ain't him!" I looked at Tay and she rolled her eyes but stayed silent. I asked her about Sweetie and I told her I would love to see her. Brenda had two other kids but I never really knew them. She said that it wasn't a good idea to see Sweetie because she never got over Stephan's molestation. Trent told me a story in one of his letters that shook my soul every time I recalled it. Stephan would take Sweetie out of town with him. He would take Sweetie panties off, make her sit with her legs open and played with her down there while he was driving. One time an eighteen wheeler was driving by and looked down in the car and saw what he was doing and just shook his head. Brenda told me that her baby had not been the same since. She had several emotional break downs and had been in and out of mental institutions since she was a child. TEARS!

CHAPTER THIRTEEN

MOTHERS, Let us have a conversation

I never researched the psychological or statistical views of my story. I was not concerned with stats, numbers, opinions or evaluations. I took you inside my nightmare to extend a better view. My goal is to explain the mentality of a child so a mother can better understand and deal with her child as it relates to sexual molestation.

RIPLEY'S BELIEVE IT OR NOT

A young child is not knowledgeable about anything in this life. They haven't experienced many things and they rely on adults to teach them the difference between wrong and right. If they have an adult in their life that introduces them to wrong doing, they don't have the experience to filter the situation. You may think that I don't need to say this but it needs to be said. You have MOTHERS that blame their 9 year old daughter of being fast and enticing their boyfriend when he molests her. Who is the adult here? He is the adult who made the decision to move forward with this crime that is why he goes to jail and the child goes to counseling. Believe it or not that mother is jealous that he wanted that little girl and views her as any other women on the street that he cheated with. MOTHER, CHECK YOURSELF! Your child was molested because that's who he was and it was his intentions along. This is not the first or the last time he will molest a child as long as ignorant, unaware mothers exist and continually allow him access to their children. He has been planning this from the start by gradually offering to watch her, saying suggestive remarks to her, touching her inappropriately, rewarding her, telling her it is ok or threatening and scaring her. Then he starts working on the mother by suggesting negative observations to her, acting as though the child is giving suggestive attention to him and he is insulted. He makes comments like she is fast and the next thing you know the mother is saying the same thing about her own child. The child that heard this come out of your mouth looks at it as betrayal. Yes, this needs to be said because it happens more often you think.

BFF'S

If this situation has become a part of a child's life for over a period of time; like mine, this person became a part of my life for 14 years; this molester is calculating and patient. A child not knowing how people operate thinks that if a person is nice, then that makes them a good person. They don't know to listen to their first mind, the knot in their stomach or just to be suspicious period. As long as this person rewards them with toys, sweets and all the other things that are important to a child, a child will not think there is anything wrong. At this time this pervert is not causing any physical pain, they are just touching or however they get their kicks. The child will notice that when the mother is being mean and negative towards them this person can calm their mothers down and help them avoid punishment. This person then becomes the child's ally against their parent who is regarded as an adversary.

FLIPPIN' THE SCRIPT

This molester employs mind games with the child. They make the child think that there is nothing wrong with what they are doing. Everyone does it, it's perfectly normal, it's just a game and it's their little secret. After a while when the child becomes resistant for whatever reason, that's when this person **flips the script** and will say; they asked for it, they wanted it, they would get in trouble and that their parents wouldn't love them. They teach them that this is not something bad or something to be ashamed of but in return make them feel tainted. Mothers should pay close attention to the things their child will say and do. When a child does something that is not age appropriate it should be questioned intensely but calmly. This person is now manipulating your child to accommodate his needs right under your nose.

KNOWLEDGE IS POWER

MOTHERS, EDUCATE YOUR CHILD! All I knew about sex was the story of the birds and the bees which was very confusing. I remember thinking, "Birds and bees do it to each other? What does that baby look like?" Talk to your child about bad touches and good touches. Parents have a problem with talking about sex to their kids. Even though we all know **knowledge is power** we refuse to enlighten our children. THIS IS A BIG MISTAKE! I can honestly say I didn't know to tell it. By the time I knew I was so far in it, my mother was under his control and I was stuck.

CUTTING THE APRON STRINGS

You haven't noticed but this person has broken a bond between you and your child with your help. Yes, you're right, you and your child used to talk about any and everything. You've talked about another kid hitting them, kids calling them out of their name, things that hurt their feelings, made them mad and made them uncomfortable. But if you make your child feel you love this person more and that is where you loyalty lies, the communication is broken between you and your child. Never discuss your child with this person in front of the child. Never agree with negative comments about your child in front of your child. This person can use your words against you. BOND IS BROKEN! You can say what you want but no child tells their mother everything, SO STOP SAYING THAT! A child is easily intimidated; this person looks ten feet tall and scary. They can intimidate your child without putting their hands on them. Harsh words are just as effective. No one should be allowed to say anything to you about your child anyway. I don't care who they are.

UNITED FRONT

Don't ever call your child a liar in front of this person. It makes a child with limited verbal skills defend themselves against a mature, socially skilled, intelligent adult. You pull that child off to the side and calmly let him or her explain the situation. To scold your child or call them a liar in front of this person just shows that you don't listen to your child so now he can do as he pleases. You also just let your child know who you're more loyal to. By pulling your child away privately you show a united front. This person sees that you have a relationship and dialogue with your child and you will investigate to the fullest.

BETTER LATE THAN NEVER

Mothers don't believe their child if the information is revealed at a later date. UMMMMM! WHAT THE HELL DOES THAT HAVE TO DO WITH ANYTHING? We act like; as adults we never hesitated to tell things at first. Sometimes it's because you brushed it off and didn't know to tell it until something happens. Sometimes you didn't tell it out of fear or how it may be perceived at the time. Sometimes we don't tell because at that time we aren't strong enough or are too scared and one day you have the courage to tell it. Sometimes it's very sensitive because of the parties involved (uncle, brother, father, boyfriend, step father). Sometimes the child is hesitant because of the way you handle conflict.

~~~~~~~

When my oldest daughter was around elementary age if someone mistreated her she hated to tell me. The level in which I

clowned; she said I embarrassed her. She told me I got too mad
and she thought I would end up in jail so she only told me things
she couldn't hide.

~~~~~~~

A child won't tell until this person is removed from their personal space when they feel safe. A child is considered a liar or must have liked it if they didn't say something immediately.

BEEN THERE, DONE THAT

Mothers treat their young children like they have been here before or were born with life experience. They act as though their young children should have known this or known that. A child won't put importance on the same issues we would as adults. When I was going through my nightmare I put no importance on being abused. I was mad about not being able to go outside and play with my friends. I did whatever it took to get it over with so I could go back outside because as a child that was important.

MY GAME IS TIGHT

Predators are big risk takers, impulsive and they have no boundaries. "Everything done in the dark will come to light" but by then it is often too late. When someone wants to get a hold of your child; if you let them in your circle, they will. We put our kids in this situation and then get mad when it happens. It's amazing how we won't leave our purse and cell phone in the room with a man we just met but will go to work for eight hours and leave a man we barely know in our home alone with our kids.

~~~~~~~

Once I was in a crowded barbershop waiting to get my hair cut, I decided to ask the men a question. After I made sure that they fully understood under no shape, form or fashion was I accusing any of them of being a pedophile; I asked, "Combine all the relationships you've been in, all the females you were casually involved with and female acquaintances. How many of their children, could you have gotten a hold to? Every guy in the barber shop agreed and said, "All of them." SAD!

I UNDERSTAND

I know as mothers we make a lot of sacrifices to take care of our children. We are never able to falter regardless how sick, how heartbroken, how lonely or how depressed. We are expected to keep it moving. We have our own issues that we are never able to give full attention to because our focus is on the problems and issues of our children. We focus on work, paying bills, cooking, cleaning, homework and the maintenance of our lifestyles. We go without romantic partners; without loving, touching, kisses and the attention that makes us feel like women.

We do the best we can with what we have. We give all that we have inside of us and pray it's enough. For whatever reason we end up raising our children alone; whether it is due to death, they bailed, they moved on to something easier, they ran from their responsibility without a blink of the eye, without any doubt in their minds or without guilt. Mothers never get the acknowledgement that no matter how young, how scared, how confused; we remain loyal, we stay strong, WE STAYED! We are the ones that are not appreciated. We get blamed for everything, everything is our fault. We live with a lot of guilt but at the end of the day, we give up our lives and all our children do is complain. Eventually burn out becomes reality.

But let's just keep it real, a lot of mothers are just selfish and their children are options instead of priority. We sacrifice them and become selfish to have the things that we want and do. When that happens it becomes very easy for predators to sneak up on you. You close your eyes to the obvious because it's a hard pill to swallow knowing that you dropped the ball. You became neglectful, irresponsible and selfish. I honestly feel if you don't take care of your children God is not going to bless you.

~~~~~~~

NOTE TO MOTHERS: Life is a cycle, when your children are young it's your responsibility to take care of them. All the things that are so important to you, all the places you want to go and all the men that you put in front of them that you thought were so important; is not going to be so important when you're old and need some assistance. When you're old and sick and need your children to take care of you. NEWSFLASH: They will not be there!

~~~~~~~~

DENIAL

It's very necessary to mend your relationship with your child when you allow their childhood to be hijacked. Don't leave this earth without fixing this. YOU broke it so YOU fix it. If not for you, do it for your child. A person will carry this hurt, abuse and betrayal around in their heart, mind and spirit for the rest of their lives. It will affect their adult lives with such negativity. It's hard to forgive yourself when you didn't protect your child. The torture is knowing you left your child defenseless because at the time, it was all about you and you sacrificed your child for what you were trying to get or keep. These days children are actually telling their mothers and in order to hold on to a man or whatever the case may be, you allowed it to happen and you allowed it to continue.

You know what else is so hurtful? The mother can't face her fuck up so she spends years making the child feel responsible for the situation. She will show anger, have childish petty excuses as to why she didn't have control of what happened. She degrades the child and creates insecurity. By tearing down her/his character their self esteem is lowered. They treat the child like a leper. Frequently, the mother will shut down and distance herself for years sometimes forever to avoid dealing with this terrible disservice she did to her child.

I want victims to know, your mother's reaction is really how she feels about herself. She is using you for a punching bag to release all of her pinned up frustration she has inside because she feels like shit!

If a women wronged her man and he was leaving her; she would hold him by his leg being dragged across the floor as he walks out the door. She would beg him not to leave, promise to make it up to him and beg him to forgive her. So why is it that we can wrong our children and expect them to get over it without an apology. THINK ABOUT IT.

THE ROAD TO HEALING

Mothers don't give up on your relationship with your children because the situation seems too far out of hand or you feel that you have done the unforgivable. I don't know a child, no matter what they've been through, no matter how old they are who doesn't want to have a relationship with their mother. Children always need their mothers.

-You must sit down and have a conversation and you have this conversation with an open heart and mind.

-Be willing to hear the truth no matter how much it hurts. Put your anger and feelings on the back burner because this is not about you.

-Be prepared to answer some really hard questions and be as honest as you can. If you don't have an answer you might have to say that.

-Don't make excuses: You may choose not to speak because to say anything sounds like an excuse.

-This process is not going to be easy. Your emotions, ego and pride will take a beating.

-When it's your turn to speak, humble yourself and give your child a sincere apology.

-Don't be afraid to really show them your pain. They need to see that. They need to see sincerity, remorse, sorrow, embarrassment, understanding, forgiveness, grief, and defeat.

-Take responsibility for your actions and release them from their guilt.

The only way to heal is to accept what you've done, apologize to your child and ask for forgiveness and then forgive yourself.

Regardless of the reasons or excuses the point is we as mothers are responsible for our children's well being. We are their protectors, their decision makers, their teachers, we give them the first impression of themselves, we have control of their self esteem and the way they handle their insecurities. We are all they have and there is no room for selfish errors. We are allowed mistakes, no one is perfect. If you search your heart and make a decision based on what you think and feel is right at that time; then pray about it. Regardless of the outcome, you have done the best job that you could. After that, you lay your head on your pillow every night and you rest with no guilt.

CHAPTER FOURTEEN

MY MOTHER

When I was about 33 years old, my mother came by to visit me and the girls. I don't know how the subject came up but we started to talk about the nightmare I lived all by myself for so long. This was a very touchy subject. We tried to talk about it years ago but my mother always got upset and still blamed us by saying, "Well, you guys were the ones who liked him and Toni I was surprised you of all my children didn't tell me." She would always blow it off with the attitude (leave the past in the past.) We had a very strained relationship for years and it didn't seem that anything would change any time soon.

I was cooking dinner when my mother knocked on the door. We greeted each other with a hug but this hug was different. It touched my cold heart the way she held onto me. I saw sadness in her eyes. Once everything was cooking in the oven, I sat down next to her at the table in silence. She stared at me for a while. I stared back trying to read her for an answer as to why she was there without asking. I kind of had a feeling we were about to have this dreaded conversation because even though she had sadness in her eyes, I saw strength and courage. After all these years I think she was prepared to find out how her family was torn apart. I always cherished my mother. I think of all her children, I idolized her the most. I wanted to be just like her when I was a child. I told her when I was younger that I would never leave her. She called me her "joy bell" because I always kept her laughing, even till this day.

She finally spoke, she said, "Tell me what he did to you." I didn't hesitate. I started at the beginning. She listened to my nightmare without saying a word. When I was done I saw a broken woman. I saw her shame and pity. I saw her take all her emotional punches that left emotional bruises. I saw her take responsibility and blame. I saw her eyes plead for forgiveness and understanding. I saw remorse. For the first time in my life I saw my mother cry. She cried with battled emotions. She cried with defeat. My mother got up and pulled me to her and hugged me as her body shook with grief. She kissed me on my forehead and left.

That night I got on my knees and told God it was time for this to end. I asked him to release me from any anger and animosity. I thanked him for sticking with me through my storm and protecting me. I thanked him for my babies and all my blessings. That night I forgave my mother so I thanked him for giving me my mother back. AMEN.

~~~~~~~

*********A couple of years ago for her birthday we decided to buy her a television. We always get together to make sure she was treated special on her birthday by giving her something that she really wants. That year we included a letter from all her children with her gift. I included the letter on the next page that we entitled, "A love letter to Mama"*************************

A LOVE LETTER TO MAMA

To Mama,

We decided that this was a perfect time to set a couple of things straight just in case you are confused about where we stand with you. We all know that the road we travel was not an easy one but in the end it was worth the trip. One thing that you instill in us is the ability to see something positive in all situations. Though the smoke and fire when it cleared, we found a black, strong, determined women who instills in us very important qualities that made us the great women we are today.

We found through our lives that we were raised on a level that most people could not comprehend BUT WE GOT IT! You taught us the struggle so we don't crumble when things get tough. We learned the discipline of hard work and determination. We are hardworking, go-getters and we can honestly say we learned that by example; watching you do your thing with ease and grace.

We are women of honesty, integrity, character and morals. You taught us that common sense is not common and if we didn't know something or know how to do something, you gave us the skills to find out. We are responsible, strong minded individuals with pride that we carry deep inside of us that exudes beyond measure. We are all these things because we had a positive example to follow.

At this time we would like to thank you and tell you that we appreciate you for your perseverance and your dedication to the task of caring for your family with all the tools that you possessed. YOU'RE A PHENOMENAL WOMAN!

WE LOVE AND RESPECT YOU.

EPILOGUE

HOW AM I DOING?

One day I was complaining to my mother about not having the things and the life that other children have and my mother looked at me and said, "You may not have the life that other children have but you possess something that they would never comprehend." She told me I was a survivor. She gave me the example; that if all the parents left off the street and gave all the children a month's worth of food, they would mess over or waste their food and starve to death. But because I knew how to survive, I would know to ration my food to make it last all month and stay alive. My mother had a way of explaining things to me to make me understand, and I GOT IT!

~~~~~~~

I know my reality was a hard road travelled but it is MY TRUTH! Don't pity me because I don't! I have been blessed with the ability to take the worst situation and see all my blessings. Sometimes good things come from the worst situation and this is the way I view my life. I feel as though I walked through a burning building that exploded and I came out a little dirty, stinky and smoky but I was protected. I never blamed myself for my situation. I refuse to claim that bullshit.

I know my mother came out in my book like a really selfish uncaring BITCH and she was. But she gave me a lot of great qualities and that is the reason I was able to deal with my situation head on. She made me strong, able to handle situations with my eyes wide open and to face reality. I am not a follower and I have my own mind. She taught us how to organize, make no excuses, to hustle for the life that I wanted and to fight for my survival. I never had the time to fall apart. All I had time for was to figure out my next move and this is the way I handled my nightmare. If you ask me what this journey showed me about myself, if you ask me what my mother instilled in me, if you ask me to describe myself in one word, I would answer... *UNBREAKABLE!*

All I know is that I loved my babies. They needed me and I needed them. They were my focus and I really enjoy being a mother. They became my soldiers and I honor them to the highest. I don't dwell on their conception because no matter what they are my babies, my best friends and they kept me company throughout my nightmare. I'm not upset about my life because when the smoke cleared I was blessed with my girls so it's hard to wallow in my nightmare because I got something so wonderful from it, SO I FORGIVE LIFE!

I didn't write my story to mourn, I wrote my story to explain that predators exist in this world and they have many ways to prey on unsuspecting victims. They have a plan to move into your life with an agenda. As I tell my story you see how Stephan played his game, used our mothers as puppets and preyed upon their children to satisfy his sexual deviancy. He was not educated; I don't even think he had a high school education but he was smart, calculating and manipulative. He destroyed family bonds and trust to achieve his goals. I wrote this book so you could see how our mothers allowed their children to become his TARGETS! I am just an average woman with an average life. I made it through life by praying with the grace of God and common sense. I wrote this story to enlighten and to educate other possible victims. Even though I am a grown woman now I told this story *"THROUGH A CHILD'S EYES!"*

THAT WAS MY NIGHTMARE! THIS WAS MY JOURNEY!

ACKNOWLEDGEMENTS

There can be only one reason why after all my experiences I was left sane enough, emotionally stable enough and blessed with the ability to speak and people listen. I found that they really want to hear what I have to say: God is the source of everything I have become.

God has blessed me with the love and support of my children. Thank you for your unwavering faith in me. I love you and pray that you continue to give me strength to be my own person and have the foresight to see the good and the lesson in the worst situation. I pray that you continue to be proud of me and let the universe provide me with all the blessings that I'm entitled to. I want to thank you, my heavenly Father for putting people with pure hearts in my life and who truly loved me with no shame and no judgments.

To my loving family, my sisters, Gwendolyn C. Forrest and Sharrie J. Forrest who stood up for me with no fear even though they were scared to death. I love my sisters. My daughters, Tyra Kenyale and Tiffany Kyrise who became my soldiers and made my life easy by being the best two children a mother could ever pray for. They showed their appreciation by cooking, cleaning and washing so I wouldn't have to do anything but rest when I got home. They allowed me to work my two jobs to provide for us in peace. They showed appreciation for my hard work by doing well in school and staying out of trouble. I thank you for always making me feel appreciated by not whining, complaining and accepting our life as it was. I love you both with everything inside of me and I'm very proud of the young ladies/mothers you have become. I couldn't have done any of this without you. You two gave me the strength to fight for our place in this world and I will always honor you forever.

Doris B. Jackson, my second mother. I called you Dai in my story, it means beloved one of great importance. Because of you I know the feeling of a mother's love. I want to thank you for embracing my daughters and me without shame or judgment. Thank you for standing up for me when you didn't even know what you were standing up for. Everyone always said that you were never the most affectionate women but you always had a hug and kiss for me. I always felt love from you. I want to thank you for expressing pride in me. It meant the world to me when you would tell me how proud you were of me. Thank you for giving me a role model to immolate because I wanted to be the kind of mother/women you are. I love you so much and I honor you to the fullest. Thank you for being my mom.

Daphne L. Riddick, my best friend. I can't even begin with you. I think you saved my life. You were all I had since I was seven years old. I know you didn't understand what was going on with me at such a young age. You didn't even know about such evilness in this world. You were so innocent. All you knew was that I was your best friend and you loved me and we built our friendship on that. I want to thank you for being my friend at a time when I had no one. I thank you for making me happy when I was so unhappy. I thank you sharing your mom with me and never being jealous of the love she had for me. I was going through so much when we met. I was so confused and my heart was so heavy and you became my best friend and that made my soul smile. I thank you for understanding even when you didn't understand. For crying with me even when you didn't know what I was crying for and making me laugh even when I didn't have a damn thing to laugh about. I honor you as well. Thank you for being my friend at the worst part of my life.

Thelma "Nell" Mack, (R.I.P 2007), my daughters' second mother. You were such a kindred spirit with a wonderful heart. I was truly blessed with an angel. Thank you so much for being in my daughters' life and treating them like they were your very own. Thank you for being there when I had no help. Even when you moved to Louisiana, you wanted them, spent time with them and did whatever it took to stay a part of their life, (that 18 hrs drive was no joke). Thank you for your love and support. We will always love and honor you forever and ever. I would also like to thank the whole Charles family for embracing my babies and providing them with a grandmother, a grandfather and Aunties. Thank you, Nana Frances, PawPaw Jessie, Aunt Elaine, Aunt Vickie, and Aunt Sandra. Thank you Mother Mary, you were truly a blessing.

Katie Mae Rodgers, third mother. You came into my life and gave my babies and me stability. You slowed things down in my life so that I could come up with a plan. (I needed that) Everything was so crazy and I couldn't get out of my whirlwind. Thank you for being there for me when I really didn't know how I was going to provide for my babies for the rest of our life. For the first time I had someone who had my back and supported what I was trying to do. Thank you so much for taking on some of my responsibility like handling school situations so I wouldn't have to miss work. Evelyn Wilson, I can't forget about you, I know you picked up mama's slack and made it possible for things to happen for me as well, I will always appreciate both of you. Alicia Ann Rodgers, my big sister, Thank you for being tough when I needed it and compassionate when I needed that to. Thank you for all your teaching, training, and wonderful advice. You were the one who gave me my platform. Thank you for caring enough to set my feet in the right direction. I love you and will always appreciate you.

I had mothers that came in my life that didn't even know they impacted my life. I barely knew them and they didn't know me nor had any idea what I was going through but always had a kind word that made me keep pushing and I would like to honor them as well. Sarah Tolbert, (R.I.P. 2012) thank you for always having compassion in your eyes for me that told me not to be ashamed. I gravitated toward your loving motherly spirit and I felt peace. Thank you so much I really needed that. To Sandra Harris, (R.I.P. 2002) Thank you for not judging me and having a kind word for me with compliments that let me know that God was watching over me. You were part of his protection because when I periodically ran into you, you were so positive towards me that made me positive. Thank you so much. Ms. Willa Deasfernandes, we never had much to say to each other even though I came over every day to hang with Natalie. You made me comfortable enough that when I needed you, you were there. I thank you for helping me when protective service wanted to take my babies from me and you let me use your home to convince them that I was a good mother. I never forgot about that. That made you awesome in my book. Thank you for being there for me. You probably don't even remember this but I never forgot. I never forgot that you drove me all the way on the east side to pick up my prom dress even though you didn't drive on the freeway and you took all side streets. I will always remember you. Thank you.

Deanda Jene Smith, my cousin, I just wanted to mention you because you're my favorite cousin (smile). I love you, Cuz. Laverne Viola Jones, mom/ book buddy, you always treated me with love and respect. When I told you about my book, your excitement excited me. Thanks for the encouragement. Sheila Sims and Mona Bradley thank you for being my friends for over twenty years. All my love to my Dallas Design family: Margi Gray, Erroll King, Floyd Edmonds, Bershander (Sharon) Washington, Sandy McFadden and Ms. Jerri McClenic (R.I.P. 2010) and our wonderful family of clients that have showed me so much love, respect and acceptance for who I am. I have learned so much from all of you and I feel so blessed. Thank you for all your love and encouragement.

SPECIAL THANKS:

Ms Gwendolyn Biggs, MBA. Thank you so much for putting the final polish on my book. I asked you for help and you did it without hesitation. I appreciate the diligence in which you attacked my project, all your wonderful advice and genuine encouragement that you gave. It's so surreal to me that you did it without a thought or hesitation. I feel so honored to have met you.

Margi Gray, my Mentor, my Mom, my Friend. I feel so honored to have met a wonderful woman like you. You have such a kind, giving, selfless, spirit about you. You are someone that has graced my life and forever left an impression. I have learned so much from you and I appreciate the time and the attention that you set aside for me. I know you wouldn't have invested the effort in me if you didn't think I was worthy, I consider that a compliment. You are smart, funny, classy, sensitive and a force to be reckon' with all rolled up in one. You are the epitome of a strong, black independent woman and you will always have my respect. I will never forget you, Margene. I have grown into a better person and an even stronger woman because of all you represent. I will always love you forever and ever, Amen.

THERE ARE SO MANY TIMES THAT I READ A BOOK AND WISHED I COULD HAVE A CONVERSATION WITH THE AUTHOR, TO ANSWER PERPLEXING QUESTIONS. I'M GOING TO GIVE YOU AND OPPORTUNITY TO GET IT ALL OFF YOUR CHEST. THERE IS AN "ASK ME" PAGE ON MY WEBSITE www.throughachildseyes290611.com. I PROMISE TO ANSWER THEM ALL.

AUTHOR Phillis T. Forrest